JOHN 1–10

I Am the
Bread of Life

A Guided Discovery for Groups and Individuals

Kevin Perrotta

LOYOLAPRESS.
CHICAGO

LOYOLAPRESS.

3441 N. ASHLAND AVENUE
CHICAGO, ILLINOIS 60657

Imprimatur
Most Reverend Raymond E. Goedert,
M.A., S.T.L., J.C.L.
Vicar General
Archdiocese of Chicago
April 24, 2001

Nihil Obstat
Reverend John Lodge, S.S.L., S.T.D.
Censor Deputatus
April 20, 2001

The *Nihil Obstat* and *Imprimatur* are official declarations that a book is free of doctrinal and moral error. No implication is contained therein that those who have granted the *Nihil Obstat* and *Imprimatur* agree with the content, opinions, or statements expressed.

The Scripture quotations contained herein are from the New Revised Standard Version Bible: Catholic Edition, copyright © 1993 and 1989 by the Division of Christian Education of the National Council of the Churches of Christ in the U.S.A. Used by permission. All rights reserved. Subheadings in Scripture quotations have been added by the author.

The excerpt from Anthony Bloom (p. 34) is from *Courage to Pray* (New York: Paulist Press, 1973), 56.

The French text of the excerpt from St. Francis de Sales (p. 35) may be found in *Oeuvres complètes de saint François de Sales, tome iv,* "Sermons, première partie," (Paris: Louis Vivès, 1871), 123, 125–26, 130–31. Translation by Louise Perrotta. An English translation is available in *The Sermons of St. Francis de Sales for Advent and Christmas,* "Second Sunday after Epiphany" (Rockford, Ill.: Tan, 1987), 110, 112–17.

The excerpts from the writings of St. Teresa of Avila (p. 47) are from *The Book of Her Life* and *Soliloquies* in Kieran Kavanaugh, O.C.D., and Otilio Rodriguez, O.C.D., trans., *The Collected Works of St. Teresa of Avila,* vol. 1, (Washington, D.C.: I.C.S. Publications, 1976), 202, 381–82; © 1976 Washington Province of Discalced Carmelites. I.C.S. Publications, 2131 Lincoln Road, N.E., Washington, DC 20002-1199 U.S.A.

The Syriac text (with English translation) of the Odes of Solomon (pp. 48–49) can be found in James H. Charlesworth, *The Odes of Solomon* (Missoula, Mont.: Scholars Press, 1977). Translation by Kevin Perrotta.

The complete text of St. John Chrysostom's Homily 37 on the Gospel of John (p. 59) is available in Sister Thomas Aquinas Goggin, S.C.H., translator, *Saint John Chrysostom: Commentary on Saint John the Apostle and Evangelist,* The Fathers of the Church, vol. 33 (New York: Fathers of the Church, 1957), 359–67. Translation by Kevin Perrotta. The excerpt from Raymond E. Brown on the same page is from his book, *The Gospel according to John (I–XII),* The Anchor Bible, vol. 29 (New York: Doubleday, 1966), 209.

The excerpt from John Henry Newman (p. 83) is from *Parochial and Plain Sermons,* vol. 8 (London: Longman, Green, and Co., 1908), 241–43.

Interior design by Kay Hartmann/Communique Design
Illustration by Charise Mericle Harper

ISBN 0-8294-1566-1

Printed in the United States of America
    04 05 06 07 08 09 Bang 9 8 7 6 5 4 3

Contents

How to Use This Guide

You might compare the Bible to a national park. The park is so large that you could spend months, even years, getting to know it. But a brief visit, if carefully planned, can be enjoyable and worthwhile. In a few hours you can drive through the park and pull over at a handful of sites. At each stop you can get out of the car, take a short trail through the woods, listen to the wind blowing through the trees, get a feel for the place.

In this booklet we'll drive through the first half of John's Gospel, making half a dozen stops along the way. At those points we'll proceed on foot, taking a leisurely walk through the selected passages. The readings have been chosen to take us to the heart of John's portrayal of Jesus. After each discussion we'll get back in the car and take the highway to the next stop. "Between Discussions" pages summarize the portions of the Gospel that we will pass by.

This guide provides everything you need to begin exploring John, chapters 1 through 10, in six discussions—or to do a six-part exploration on your own. The introduction on page 6 will prepare you to get the most out of your reading. The weekly sections feature key passages from the Gospel, with explanations that highlight what these words mean for us today. Equally important, each section supplies questions that will launch you into fruitful discussion, helping you to both explore the Gospel for yourself and learn from one another. If you're using the booklet by yourself, the questions will spur your personal reflection.

Each discussion is meant to be a *guided discovery.*

Guided. None of us is equipped to read the Bible without help. We read the Bible *for* ourselves but not *by* ourselves. Scripture was written to be understood and applied in the community of faith. So each week "A Guide to the Reading," drawing on the work of both modern biblical scholars and Christian writers of the past, supplies background and explanations. The guide will help you grasp the message of John's Gospel. Think of it as a friendly park ranger who points out noteworthy details and explains what you're looking at so you can appreciate things for yourself.

Discovery. The purpose is for *you* to interact with John's Gospel. "Questions for Careful Reading" is a tool to help you dig into the text and examine it carefully. "Questions for Application" will help you consider what John's words mean for your life here and now. Each week concludes with an "Approach to Prayer" section that helps you respond to God's word. Supplementary "Living Tradition" and "Saints in the Making" sections offer the thoughts and experiences of Christians past and present in order to show you what the Gospel of John has meant to others—so that you can consider what it might mean for you.

How long are the discussion sessions? We've assumed you will have about an hour and a half when you get together. If you have less time, you'll find that most of the elements can be shortened somewhat.

Is homework necessary? You will get the most out of your discussions if you read the weekly material and prepare your answers to the questions in advance of each meeting. But if participants are not able to prepare, have someone read the "Guide to the Reading" section aloud to the group at the points where it occurs in the weekly material.

What about leadership? If you happen to have a world-class biblical scholar in your group, by all means ask him or her to lead the discussions. But in the absence of any professional Scripture scholars, or even accomplished biblical amateurs, you can still have a first-class Bible discussion. Choose two or three people to be facilitators, and have everyone read "Suggestions for Bible Discussion Groups" before beginning (page 92).

Does everyone need a guide? a Bible? Everyone in the group will need their own copy of this booklet. It contains the sections of John that are discussed, so a Bible is not absolutely necessary—but each participant will find it useful to have one. You should have at least one Bible on hand for your discussions. (See page 96 for recommendations.)

How do we get started? Before you begin, take a look at the suggestions for Bible discussion groups (page 92) or individuals (page 95).

Deep Waters

S ome years ago our family camped on the Bruce Peninsula, a
finger of land separating Lake Huron and Georgian Bay in
Canada. When you vacation with preschool children, you become keenly sensitive to the drop-off in any nearby body of water.
Looking at a lake, the fisherman sees walleye and trout habitat;
the parent sees inclined planes leading down into a drowning hazard.
That year we had a range of drop-offs to choose from. Yards from
our camper was Cyprus Lake: a skimpy beach falling off rather
sharply into dark water. Across the highway were shallow sand flats
stretching far out into Lake Huron. A two-year-old like our Meggie
could toddle a hundred feet through warm puddles without even
getting her swimsuit wet. On the other side of the peninsula was
Tobermory, where white dolomite cliffs descend vertically into the
deep cobalt blue waters of Georgian Bay. Registering a ten on the
parental ten-point drop-off scale, Tobermory is, in fact, the finest
natural harbor in North America.

To my mind, the Gospel of John is the Tobermory of the
Bible. John provides no gradual introduction to his subject. Verse 1
is a total drop-off. Beginning to read is stepping off a cliff and
plunging into profound mystery: "In the beginning was the Word,
and the Word was with God, and the Word was God." Deep waters
indeed! John tells us about the decisive encounter between God
and the human race in a richly symbolic style that is appropriate
for his subject but not always easy to read. Like the waters of
Georgian Bay, the Gospel of John has hidden depths. It is easy for
the reader to feel overwhelmed.

As we begin to explore these deep waters, it will
be helpful to have an idea of John's basic message. Quite simply, in
John's view, we human beings need God. We need God's light to
illuminate our lives, his power to energize us. But for the most part
we are only dimly conscious of this need because we are locked
into this-world-only thinking. We spend our lives going to and fro,
seeking one thing after another, preoccupied with meeting our
material and social needs. We are inclined to regard God as the
provider of earthly blessings rather than the source of something

much more important. And, of course, we are also inclined to disregard God and pursue our own agendas.

John tells us how God attempted to break through the barrier of our earthly thinking by entering into our world personally. He became one of us. Having become an insider in our world, God-as-one-of-us presented himself as the one who can transform our lives in ways we can hardly imagine. To help people glimpse the superlative life he offered, he cared for this-worldly needs in extraordinary ways. He miraculously produced wine and bread and healed paralysis and blindness. By these marvels he encouraged people to let go of their preoccupation with the needs of earthly life and to accept him as the source of a more-than-earthly life. John calls these marvels "signs"—pointers indicating that God-as-one-of-us offered a life immune to deterioration or loss, sickness or death.

Unfortunately, the claims of God-as-one-of-us did not make sense to people confined by earthbound thinking. His offer too far exceeded the worldly sphere in which they were seeking happiness. The very idea that God might appear as a man who walked down the street alongside everyone else offended their religious sensibilities. While they admitted that the claimant exercised remarkable powers, they failed to recognize his divine identity. Before long a few people ganged up on him and killed him. Yet, John declares, by letting himself fall victim to death, God-as-one-of-us broke death's power. Rising from the dead, he began to fill people's need for God. Ultimately, he will reverse the death of men and women and bring them into God's presence forever.

I have been speaking of John's story as though it lacked any historical context. In fact, it took place in the early first century in Roman-occupied Palestine. John's story concerns Jesus of Nazareth, who died in Jerusalem around the year 30. Because Jesus and John were first-century Palestinian Jews, John's account reflects the culture of that time and place. To understand his account, it is helpful to consider the worldview and expectations of Jewish people in first-century Palestine.

Like other Jews of his time, John is convinced that his people, Israel, have been the focus of God's activity in history.

While in his day the fortunes of the Jewish people are at low ebb, John and many of his fellow Jews believe that God is not finished with Israel. In their view, God's merciful revelation of himself in the past holds the promise of greater mercy in the future.

There are many strands in the Jewish understanding of God's activity in the world; one that is especially important for John involves a word that he never actually uses but that lies just beneath the surface of his Gospel. That word is *wisdom*.

In Jewish thought, God brought the universe into existence through a powerful act of wisdom (Proverbs 3:19–20; 8:22–31). But among God's human creatures, something went terribly wrong almost from the start. A false wisdom intruded, luring people away from reliance on God's good intentions and obedience to him (Genesis 3:1–7). Humans pursued knowledge apart from God's purposes; they became clever in advancing their own interests at one another's expense. This false wisdom had terrible results. Humankind became subject to death (Genesis 3:22–24). People became deluded about the purpose of their lives.

God never abandoned men and women to the pseudo-wisdom—foolishness, really—into which they had wandered. He offered true wisdom—the wisdom founded on "fear of the Lord," that is, trusting obedience to him (Job 28:28; Wisdom 7:22–8:1). God made this wisdom especially accessible to his people Israel (Wisdom 10–11), above all in their inspired writings (Baruch 3:9–4:4; Sirach 24:8–12, 23–29).

The sages of Israel entertained an imaginative picture of wisdom (Sirach 24) as a savvy, wealthy, and attractive woman who goes around town looking for a man willing to come and dine at her table, marry her, and devote himself to her (Proverbs 3:13–18; 8:1–21; 9:1–6; Wisdom 8). This poetic image of Lady Wisdom expressed the conviction that God comes to each of us in a personal way to show us how to live, to share his life with us, to bring us joy.

To this tradition of reflection on wisdom John adds the climactic chapter. His message is that behind the metaphor of Lady Wisdom is a real divine person who has become a human being, Jesus of Nazareth. Jesus is not simply a man who *has* God's wisdom; he is Wisdom in person, the Wisdom through which God brought all things into existence. In John's Gospel, Jesus declares that he brings "the truth." By *truth* he means more than "a statement that matches reality"; here *truth* means God's revelation of himself. Jesus himself *is* the truth, because he is the perfect image of God (14:7–9; in this booklet all Scripture citations refer to the Gospel of John unless otherwise noted). He is the divine Wisdom in human form. Calling us back from false wisdom, this Wisdom has come to enlighten us and restore to us the life for which we were created.

Rather than using the word *wisdom*, John employs a related term. He calls Jesus the "Word" of God (1:1–15). In the biblical tradition, God's "word" and his "wisdom" are closely associated (compare Proverbs 8:22–31 and Psalm 33:6, Wisdom 8:1 and Psalm 147:15–18). By calling Jesus God's "Word," John does not mean that he is God's speech. It would be more accurate to say that Jesus is God's "thought." Yet *word,* unlike *wisdom,* does suggest something communicative. To talk about God's "Word" implies that God is naturally self-expressive. "A word exists to say something," Father Francis Moloney observes. By speaking of God's "Word," John suggests that from the depths of God's being arises a desire to reveal himself to us, to give us his life. This desire is so deep and strong that God has spoken his Word into our world. His Word, the perfect expression of himself, has become a human being, bridging the chasm between creator and creature.

Having entered into our world, the Word had one central message: "Here I am!" His priority was to lead people to recognize him so that they could receive the life he offered. John shows us that in everything he said and did, Jesus pointed to himself as the source of divine life. In speeches and conversations, through symbolic actions, by miraculous signs, and finally by a voluntary death, Jesus declared that he is God's Son. He presented himself as the one who perfectly reveals God because he alone has come from God. He is God's agent, totally authorized to carry out God's life-giving will, because he is one with God.

In theory, God's dealings with the people of Israel prepared them to welcome his Word when he appeared. Jesus declared that "the scriptures . . . testify on my behalf. . . . If you believed Moses, you would believe me, for he wrote about me" (5:39, 46). In practice, earthbound thinking got in the way. Sin and the desire not to take an unpopular stand proved to be barriers against accepting Jesus. Many of the religious leaders held an understanding of Jewish tradition that could not accommodate Jesus' claim that he was God's Son, whom God had sent into the world as his unique representative. There was also an element of self-interest in the religious leaders' failure to accept Jesus. Jesus presented himself as an expression of God that so far surpassed God's previous dealings with Israel that it overshadowed Jewish rituals and festivals, temple and law. Those with the greatest stake in that existing order had strong motivation for denying that Jesus was who he said he was.

This brings us to the subject of the Jews in John's Gospel. Jesus himself and most of the people in the Gospel are Jewish. Yet John generally uses the term *the Jews* more narrowly to refer to those Jews who did not accept Jesus, especially the religious leaders. For example, although the crowd of people who come to Jerusalem to celebrate a feast are themselves all Jews, John writes that they are afraid of "the Jews" (7:13)—meaning that they are afraid of the Jewish leaders who oppose Jesus.

John's confusing way of speaking may stem from historical developments that occurred between the time of Jesus and the final editing of the Gospel, perhaps around the year 90. Of the various forms of Judaism in first-century Palestine, only two survived the Roman repression of the great Jewish rebellion (A.D. 66–70). One was the Pharisaic form, which became the basis of all later forms of Judaism. The other was Christianity. By the year 90, these two forms of Judaism had begun to go their separate ways. Jews who followed the Pharisaic path and did not accept Jesus as the Messiah continued to call themselves Jews. Jews who had become followers of Jesus ceased calling themselves Jews (they called themselves Christians), even though they saw themselves in continuity with historic Israel. Thus by John's day the term *the Jews* had become synonymous with "Jews who do not recognize Jesus as the Messiah." In his Gospel, John projects this usage back into the time of Jesus. Consequently John's negative portrayal of "the Jews" is a criticism of certain Jewish leaders of the time, not a negative picture of Judaism itself or of Jewish people in general.

John does not suggest that those Jews who misunderstand and reject Jesus do so *because they are Jews*. Their unbelief stems from factors that are shared by all people (for example, see 3:19–21; 5:40–44; 7:24; 8:15, 44–47). John uses *the Jews* to represent the world that does not receive Jesus. For example, John's statement that "the Jews" seek to kill Jesus (7:1) is parallel with the statement that "the world" hates Jesus (7:7). In some Catholic parishes it is the custom at Holy Week to read the narrative of Jesus' arrest and execution in dramatic form, with the whole congregation speaking the part of "the Jews" who seek Jesus' death. This is very much in accord with John's portrayal, for he uses *the Jews* as the representatives of all of us to the degree that we fail to believe in Jesus.

Neither John nor Jesus criticizes Judaism as incorrect or mistaken. Although we may infer that Jesus disagreed with some of the Pharisees' oral traditions about how to keep the Sabbath, this itself was already a topic of disagreement *among* Jews in the first century. Jesus declares that "salvation is from the Jews" (4:22). John portrays Jesus as the greater gift that completes the gift that God gave to Israel through Moses (1:16–17).

It bears emphasis that the negative depiction of "the Jews" in John's Gospel provides absolutely no basis for Christians to hold a negative view of either Judaism or Jewish people. Tragically, John's Gospel has in the past been perverted into a rationale for anti-Semitism. This misunderstanding has been condemned in the strongest terms by the modern Church (*Declaration on the Relationship of the Church to Non-Christian Religions,* section 4).

John's Gospel is quite different from the Gospels of Matthew, Mark, and Luke. Compared to the other Gospel writers,

John devotes much less attention to Jesus' teaching about how his followers should live; he narrates fewer incidents in Jesus' life. John focuses on Jesus' proclamation of his identity. To some extent these differences among the Gospels reflect different traditions of oral teaching among the early Christians. The question of who wrote the Gospel of John has long been debated by scholars. But whoever the main author was, John's Gospel apparently represents a line of tradition largely independent of the other Gospels. Thus it provides a historical testimony to the events of Jesus' life that complements the testimony of the other Gospels. At the same time, the author, through decades of pondering and prayer, had come to a unique vision of Jesus which affected the whole way he told of Jesus' life. John shows us the same Jesus we read about in the other Gospels, but viewed from a different angle, an angle that emphasizes Jesus as Wisdom incarnate.

The author of John's Gospel is not identified within the Gospel. From the second century, a tradition identifying the author as John the son of Zebedee and brother of James (Matthew 4:21) has been accepted throughout the Church. Within the Gospel, it seems clear that the account is based on the testimony of a disciple who goes unnamed but is referred to as "the one whom Jesus loved" (13:23; 19:26, 35; 21:20–24). Whether this "beloved disciple" is John the son of Zebedee is questioned today by many scholars. For example, why would John the son of Zebedee omit from his own Gospel so many incidents involving himself that are included in the other Gospels, such as Jesus' transfiguration and his agony in the garden (Mark 9:2; 14:33)? But uncertainty over the name of the author does not affect the Gospel's reliability or inspiration. Whatever the name of the beloved disciple, he was close to Jesus and was guided by the Spirit to compose his account. Guided by the same Spirit, the Church recognized his Gospel as an authentic portrait of Jesus. While acknowledging the questions that scholars may raise, for simplicity in this booklet we will call the author John.

John makes small details bear a heavy weight of meaning. Some of the depth and complexity of his narrative stems from this. An analogy for the way John composed his account is the way a contemporary illustrator might use a computer to create a poster. The illustrator photographs actual people and events and then tranfers the photos into her computer. Bringing up the photographic images on her computer screen, she trims, tints, and positions them and combines them with drawings and lettering. The result of her labors is a composite in which the photo fragments have taken on a symbolic quality that creates a mood and conveys a message. Similarly, John has selected quotations, actions, and objects from Jesus' life and has reshaped them into a narrative in which they function as symbols and as allusions to other biblical texts.

As a result, John's account of Jesus is both simple and profound. It calls for slow, careful reading. Individual statements of Jesus, even individual words, stand out and seem to interrupt the flow of the story, requiring us to stop and ponder. The more attentively we read, the more aware we become of deeper levels of meaning. Should we be surprised? John is dealing with something so big that no human mind can comprehend it: the human, earthly life of the Word of God, God's offer of divine life to human creatures.

We need to make room for this Gospel. If we are to hear and understand what John tells us about Jesus, we need to push back our daily preoccupations to create a zone of inner quietness and receptivity. Jesus tells his opponents, "There is no place in you for my word" (8:37). Is there a place in us for his word? As we begin John's Gospel, we would do well to consider when and where we can make a little quiet in our busy days for meditative reading and rereading. A prayer in the Byzantine liturgy offers us a word of encouragement for beginning the Gospel of John in the right frame of mind: "Let us now set aside all earthly cares, so that we may welcome the Lord of All."

WITH GOD BEFORE TIME BEGAN

Questions to Begin

15 minutes
Use a question or two to get warmed up for the reading.

1 What is your favorite opening scene in a book or movie?

2 If you had to choose someone to describe you to people who had never met you, who would it be? Why would you choose that person?

Opening the Bible

5 minutes
Read the passage aloud. Let individuals take turns reading paragraphs.

The Reading: John 1:1–34

An Awesome Identity

1 In the beginning was the Word, and the Word was with God, and the Word was God. 2 He was in the beginning with God. 3 All things came into being through him, and without him not one thing came into being. What has come into being 4 in him was life, and the life was the light of all people. 5 The light shines in the darkness, and the darkness did not overcome it.

6 There was a man sent from God, whose name was John. 7 He came as a witness to testify to the light, so that all might believe through him. 8 He himself was not the light, but he came to testify to the light. 9 The true light, which enlightens everyone, was coming into the world.

10 He was in the world, and the world came into being through him; yet the world did not know him. 11 He came to what was his own, and his own people did not accept him. 12 But to all who received him, who believed in his name, he gave power to become children of God, 13 who were born, not of blood or of the will of the flesh or of the will of man, but of God.

14 And the Word became flesh and lived among us, and we have seen his glory, the glory as of a father's only son, full of grace and truth. 15 (John testified to him and cried out, "This was he of whom I said, 'He who comes after me ranks ahead of me because he was before me.'") 16 From his fullness we have all received, grace upon grace. 17 The law indeed was given through Moses; grace and truth came through Jesus Christ. 18 No one has ever seen God. It is God the only Son, who is close to the Father's heart, who has made him known.

The First to Acknowledge Him

19 This is the testimony given by John when the Jews sent priests and Levites from Jerusalem to ask him, "Who are you?" 20 He confessed and did not deny it, but confessed, "I am not the Messiah." 21 And they asked him, "What then? Are you Elijah?" He said, "I am not." "Are you the prophet?" He answered, "No." 22 Then they said to him, "Who are you? Let us have an answer for those who sent us. What do you say about yourself?" 23 He said, "I am the voice of one crying out

in the wilderness, 'Make straight the way of the Lord,'" as the prophet Isaiah said.

²⁴ Now they had been sent from the Pharisees. ²⁵ They asked him, "Why then are you baptizing if you are neither the Messiah, nor Elijah, nor the prophet?" ²⁶ John answered them, "I baptize with water. Among you stands one whom you do not know, ²⁷ the one who is coming after me; I am not worthy to untie the thong of his sandal." ²⁸ This took place in Bethany across the Jordan where John was baptizing.

²⁹ The next day he saw Jesus coming toward him and declared, "Here is the Lamb of God who takes away the sin of the world! ³⁰ This is he of whom I said, 'After me comes a man who ranks ahead of me because he was before me.' ³¹ I myself did not know him; but I came baptizing with water for this reason, that he might be revealed to Israel." ³² And John testified, "I saw the Spirit descending from heaven like a dove, and it remained on him. ³³ I myself did not know him, but the one who sent me to baptize with water said to me, 'He on whom you see the Spirit descend and remain is the one who baptizes with the Holy Spirit.' ³⁴ And I myself have seen and have testified that this is the Son of God."

Questions for Careful Reading

10 minutes
Choose questions according to your interest and time.

1 For what reasons has the Word come into the world? Cite specific statements in the Gospel text.

2 Compare John 1:1 and Genesis 1:1. What are the similarities and differences? What might be John's reason for starting his Gospel in a way so like the start of Genesis?

3 Approximately what span of time is covered from verse 1 to verse 29?

4 Judging from this reading, what sort of expectations did people have regarding John the Baptist?

5 In what way is the Word life for us? What does it mean to be begotten by God? This reading raises many questions. What questions does the reading raise in your mind? Discuss them now, and jot them down for reference later in your reading.

A Guide to the Reading

If participants have not read this section already, read it aloud.
Otherwise go on to "Questions for Application."

If you were a first-century Galilean Jew and saw Jesus walking with his disciples through the marketplace of a town or listened to him speaking to a crowd, you would have known from his language and accent that he was a local Galilean. If you spent time with him, paid close attention to his teaching, and observed the miracles he performed, you might reach the conclusion that he was an agent of God, a special prophet, or even the one promised by God who would establish his reign on earth—the Messiah. If you then shared your conclusion with the John who wrote the Gospel, he would tell you, "Right! Jesus *is* the Messiah. But he is infinitely more than that." In the first eighteen verses of his Gospel, John presents the "infinitely more" of Jesus.

To understand Jesus, John says, you must first know something about God. There is only one God, but within God there is a mysterious relationship. God's thought, or wisdom, or "Word," is not just a feature or expression of God, but a person. This person has always been in an intimate relationship with God: he is always "turned toward God" (as "the Word was with God" could be translated—1:1). Yet while this person is distinct from God, he is not different from God: "the Word was God" (1:1), in other words, "what God was, the Word was."

By telling us this, John thrusts us into the profound mystery of God's being. He gives us a glimpse of the Trinity. His purpose, however, is not to explore God's inner life but to clarify something about what we might call God's "outer life"—his creating the universe and caring for his creatures. John's point is that this person who is eternally in an intimate relationship with God, who is indeed God, through whom God has brought everything into existence, is the same person who walked through Galilean villages as Jesus of Nazareth. *That* is the "infinitely more" about Jesus that is crucial for understanding him. It means, as scholar C. K. Barrett comments, that "the deeds and words of Jesus are the deeds and words of God."

John's opening declaration reaches a climax in verse 14. "The Word became flesh and lived among us." The Word, who fully expresses God's purposes and presence, became one of us. No more perfect expression of love is imaginable. God became like us and entered into our human life, with all its difficulties and limitations. In his human existence, the Word of God lived most of his life as an ordinary person in a tiny village, working and recreating and praying with his peasant relatives and neighbors. Missionaries who go to live among the poor whom they serve, adopting their lifestyle—one thinks of Mother Teresa's Missionaries of Charity—offer merely a faint reflection of the love by which the Word of God came and took his place among us.

Jesus' mission is to reveal God to us and share God's life with us (1:12–13, 18). This revealing and sharing of life—and the rejection that it will meet (1:10–11)—will be John's subject in the chapters ahead.

John the Baptist first appears in verses 6 to 8 and 15 and becomes the focus of attention in verses 19 to 34. John was a greatly revered figure, which is why the religious leaders expressed an interest in him (1:19, 24). Yet John insists that he is simply a pointer toward someone much greater than himself—someone who was "before" him (1:30). John's listeners may not have understood what this meant—but we, who have read the first three verses, understand just how "before" John Jesus was!

John asserts that this greater one will take away sins (1:29). This means both that Jesus will forgive sins and that he will carry out God's end-time conquest of evil in the world (compare 1 John 3:5, 8). He will also baptize with the Spirit (1:33), which means that he will immerse us in the life of God.

Verses 29 to 34 show that John receives occasional guidance from God. The Gospel will portray Jesus as someone who always knows God's will. During his entire earthly life Jesus continues in intimate love with his Father—"close to the Father's heart" (1:18)—just as when he was "with God" (1:1) before entering into time.

Questions for Application

40 minutes
Choose questions according to your interest and time.

1 Someone stands among you whom you do not recognize! (See 1:26.) Where can we look to see Jesus today? How can we recognize his presence in our lives? in the Church? in the world?

2 In what way have you experienced Jesus as the light of your life? (See 1:4.) What darkness in your life needs his light?

3 What difference does it make to you that God actually became a human being in Jesus? How would your life be different if he had not come? How should his coming in the flesh affect your relationship with him?

4 Verses 12 and 13 speak about our need for God to do something for us that goes beyond what we can do for ourselves. When have you been especially aware of this need? How did you experience God's grace in that situation?

5 In what ways does your life point people toward Jesus? What could you change in how you live or speak so that your life would point to him more effectively?

6 Perhaps for private reflection rather than discussion: What does it mean for you that the Lamb of God who takes away sins has come to you? Where do you need him to overcome the power of evil in your life? What does this reading say about the trust you can place in him in this area of your life?

"Don't be afraid of silences: some questions take time to answer and some people need time to gather courage to speak."

Whitney Kuniholm, *John: The Living Word,* A Fisherman Bible Study Guide

Approach to Prayer

15 minutes
Use this approach—or create your own!

♦ The prologue of John's Gospel has been used as a blessing (for centuries it was prayed as a final blessing at the end of the Latin Mass). In the Byzantine liturgy it is read aloud at Easter in four languages as a solemn proclamation of the victory of God's light and love over all darkness and evil. Make it your own prayer of blessing and proclamation of God's love. Let someone in the group slowly and prayerfully read aloud verses 1 through 5, 9 through 14, and 16 through 18. Allow a few moments of silent reflection. Then end by praying together the Our Father.

A Living Tradition

The Liturgical Coming of the Word

This section is a supplement for individual reading.

The Mass focuses on the end of Jesus' life. The eucharistic prayer recalls his death and resurrection. The words of institution—"This is my body . . . my blood"—recall his last meal with his disciples. Through these sacramental words, by the power of the Spirit, bread and wine are transformed into Jesus himself. He shares with us this final meal of his earthly life as the celebration of his sacrificial, covenant-making death.

But what of the beginning of Jesus' life: does the Mass contain any memorial of it? Certainly it does so implicitly. The celebration of his human death and resurrection implies his having become a human being. In addition, some forms of the liturgy contain an explicit representation of the entrance of the Word into the world. Quite fittingly, this liturgical expression is in the form of an entrance ceremony.

The most impressive of these entrance ceremonies is found in the Byzantine liturgy, which is used by Eastern Orthodox and also by some Catholics, mainly of Slavic or Arabic background. After opening prayers, the priest and deacon, holding up the Gospel book, leave the sanctuary and make a procession into the church and back to the sanctuary. The Gospel book represents Christ; the procession represents his coming into the world. As priest and deacon proceed, the congregation sings an ancient prayer celebrating the incarnation of the Word. The West Syriac liturgy, used by Catholics and some other Christians in the Near East, has a similar entrance procession, during which priest and people sing an alternating prayer in praise of Christ, who was "pleased in his kindness to come for the life and redemption of all."

The Roman liturgy, which most Catholics use, has no elaborate ceremony symbolizing the Incarnation. But it is an accepted practice for the lector or other person to carry the Gospel book aloft in the entrance procession at the beginning of Mass. Seeing the Gospel book, which represents Christ, making this solemn entrance, anyone who remembers the opening of John's Gospel might feel like crying out, "Hail to you, Word through whom all things came to be! Hail to you, Word made flesh for us!"

Between Discussions

S ince we are not skipping any of John's Gospel between Weeks 1 and 2, we have a chance here to go back and give a closer examination to the portion we just read. It rewards rereading.

Scholars offer various analyses of the structure of verses 1 to 18. It is possible that John has organized his presentation of the Incarnation in waves, which come to shore in verses 4 through 5, 9 through 11, 14, and 17 through 18. Or perhaps John proceeds chronologically. If so, everything before verse 14 is part of the build-up to the Incarnation. In this case, verses 4 and 5 may refer to the presence of God's wisdom in the world even before the Word became flesh—perhaps in the sense of God's grace and truth made available to all people, in every time and place.

Biblical scholar Raymond E. Brown suggests that verses 4 and 5 allude to the biblical account of creation. At the beginning, through his Word, God created eternal life for human beings, sym- bolized by the tree of life (Genesis 2:9). Even though the devil then deflected humans from that life (Genesis 3), the darkness of the tempter has not destroyed it. That eternal life intended for human beings continues to shine.

Verses 7 and 8 give us an example of the layering of mean- ing that is typical of John's writing. In Jewish tradition, *light* was a term for the coming Messiah and the last days (Isaiah 9:1–2; 42:6; 60:1–2). Yet Jesus is more than the Messiah. He is the light of God, the source of life for human beings.

Verse 13 speaks of the "flesh." In John, *flesh* is not matter in contrast to spirit, or body in contrast to soul. "Flesh" is our whole humanity—our good yet weak and mortal human life that needs to be completed by the gift of heavenly life. Far from being evil, the "flesh" is so good, so loved by God, that the Word of God has entered into it (1:14). Nothing could more powerfully demon- strate the value of human life.

Jesus' disciples "have seen his glory" (1:14). They have seen the beauty and radiance of God in the actions and speech of the man, Jesus of Nazareth. But John is not merely reporting on a past event. He is writing the Gospel—that is, good news—so that we too might see Jesus' glory and share in the gift he has brought. (Where do we see his glory today?)

"Grace upon grace" (1:16) is difficult to interpret. Most likely it refers to God's "grace," or "gift," of the Mosaic covenant and to the even greater "gift" of his covenant through Jesus. Thus it might be translated "a gift in place of a gift" or "love in place of love." The magnificent gift of the Mosaic law is surpassed by an even greater gift of love. In the next verse, "grace and truth" means "the gift of truth": Jesus is the true revelation of God himself and of God's mysterious plan of salvation.

In Jewish tradition, various holy people (Enoch, Moses, Baruch, Daniel), were thought to have been taken into heaven to receive revelations of God. John makes the point that none of these actually saw God face-to-face (1:18). These sightseers who went "up" into the heavenly realm only caught glimpses of God. But now the Word, who knows God intimately, has come "down" from heaven to reveal him to the world. Only Jesus reveals God because he alone has actually seen him (compare 3:11; 5:37; 6:46; 14:7–10).

Thus John expresses a profound appreciation of what God has done in the past in Israel. But he speaks of a revelation of God that so far surpasses the Jewish past that, as we will see, the revelation will be difficult for those who are rooted in that tradition to accept.

John's Gospel has something of the character of a trial. Jesus makes claims about himself that provoke other people to accuse him of putting himself on a par with God. Then Jesus calls various witnesses to his defense. Here at the beginning of the Gospel, even before Jesus himself arrives on the scene, the first witness appears—John the Baptist. Notice the courtroom terminology: "witness," "testimony" (1:7, 19, 20). His solemn declaration (1:20) is like the oath of a modern witness to tell "the truth, the whole truth, and nothing but the truth."

THE FIRST SIGN

Questions to Begin

15 minutes
Use a question or two to get warmed up for the reading.

1 If you could spend the night at the home of anyone you chose, whose home would it be? Why?

2 What do you like and what do you dislike about weddings and wedding receptions?

5 minutes
*Read the passage aloud. Let individuals take turns reading
paragraphs.*

The Reading: John 1:35–2:12

Finding and Following

35 The next day John again was standing with two of his disciples,
36 and as he watched Jesus walk by, he exclaimed, "Look, here is the
Lamb of God!" 37 The two disciples heard him say this, and they followed Jesus. 38 When Jesus turned and saw them following, he said to
them, "What are you looking for?" They said to him, "Rabbi" (which
translated means Teacher), "where are you staying?" 39 He said to
them, "Come and see." They came and saw where he was staying,
and they remained with him that day. It was about four o'clock in the
afternoon. 40 One of the two who heard John speak and followed him
was Andrew, Simon Peter's brother. 41 He first found his brother
Simon and said to him, "We have found the Messiah" (which is translated Anointed). 42 He brought Simon to Jesus, who looked at him
and said, "You are Simon son of John. You are to be called Cephas"
(which is translated Peter).

    43 The next day Jesus decided to go to Galilee. He found Philip
and said to him, "Follow me." 44 Now Philip was from Bethsaida, the
city of Andrew and Peter. 45 Philip found Nathanael and said to him,
"We have found him about whom Moses in the law and also the
prophets wrote, Jesus son of Joseph from Nazareth." 46 Nathanael
said to him, "Can anything good come out of Nazareth?" Philip said
to him, "Come and see." 47 When Jesus saw Nathanael coming toward
him, he said of him, "Here is truly an Israelite in whom there is no
deceit!" 48 Nathanael asked him, "Where did you get to know me?"
Jesus answered, "I saw you under the fig tree before Philip called
you." 49 Nathanael replied, "Rabbi, you are the Son of God! You are
the King of Israel!" 50 Jesus answered, "Do you believe because I told
you that I saw you under the fig tree? You will see greater things than
these." 51 And he said to him, "Very truly, I tell you, you will see
heaven opened and the angels of God ascending and descending upon
the Son of Man."

Wedding Reception Rescue

2:1 On the third day there was a wedding in Cana of Galilee, and the
mother of Jesus was there. 2 Jesus and his disciples had also been

invited to the wedding. ³ When the wine gave out, the mother of Jesus said to him, "They have no wine." ⁴ And Jesus said to her, "Woman, what concern is that to you and to me? My hour has not yet come." ⁵ His mother said to the servants, "Do whatever he tells you." ⁶ Now standing there were six stone water jars for the Jewish rites of purification, each holding twenty or thirty gallons. ⁷ Jesus said to them, "Fill the jars with water." And they filled them up to the brim. ⁸ He said to them, "Now draw some out, and take it to the chief steward." So they took it. ⁹ When the steward tasted the water that had become wine, and did not know where it came from (though the servants who had drawn the water knew), the steward called the bridegroom ¹⁰ and said to him, "Everyone serves the good wine first, and then the inferior wine after the guests have become drunk. But you have kept the good wine until now." ¹¹ Jesus did this, the first of his signs, in Cana of Galilee, and revealed his glory; and his disciples believed in him.

¹² After this he went down to Capernaum with his mother, his brothers, and his disciples; and they remained there a few days.

Questions for Careful Reading

10 minutes
Choose questions according to your interest and time.

---

1 What impression of Jesus do you get from this reading? Does he seem to be a person who is easy to get to know? Why or why not?

---

2 If what Nathanael says in 1:46 were said today, what modern place could be substituted for "Nazareth"?

---

3 Do the math: how much wine did Jesus create? In today's terms, how many bottles would that be?

---

4 Why would people serve the good wine first?

---

5 Considering what Jesus says in 2:4, why does Mary say what she does in 2:5? Why does Jesus do what he does in 2:7–8?

A Guide to the Reading

*If participants have not read this section already, read it aloud.
Otherwise go on to "Questions for Application."*

All the Gospels show Jesus gathering disciples at the beginning of his public life. In the other Gospels, Jesus calls his disciples; here, for the most part, they seek him out (1:37, 42, 45–47). These men have already been looking for God, wanting to connect with God's activity in the world. They are so serious about their search for God that they have left home and joined John the Baptist (1:35). This puts them in the right time and place for meeting Jesus.

Jesus speaks his first words in the Gospel: "What are you looking for?" (1:38). It is his question to us, as we read about him. Are we reading the Gospel merely to satisfy our curiosity? Or are we looking for real wisdom, for a better kind of life, for God? The men's response to Jesus implies that, rather than wanting any favor or the answer to any particular question, they want the opportunity to get to know him. This is a desire that Jesus is immediately willing to grant (1:39).

Andrew seems to be a very quick learner (1:41). So does Philip, who declares that Jesus is the culmination of everything God has been doing with his people Israel throughout history (1:45). Even brief contact with Jesus leads these men to perceive that Jesus is an agent of God. But in light of the beginning of the Gospel (1:1–18) they are still a long way from grasping all that he is. Throughout John's Gospel we meet people who come to a true but incomplete recognition of who Jesus really is. Are we like them?

There are various explanations, none entirely satisfactory, for the significance of Nathanael's sitting under a fig tree (1:48). But Jesus' knowledge of people, seen here for the first time, is a characteristic that John emphasizes throughout the Gospel.

Jesus' promise (1:51) alludes to Genesis 28:12, where Jacob has a dream in which he sees angels and a ladder connecting heaven and earth. Jesus means that he himself is the point of contact between heaven and earth, the point where God reveals himself.

The numbering of the days leading up to the visit to Cana (1:29, 35, 43; 2:1) is a drumroll, alerting us to the importance of what is about to occur. The series of days may allude to the seven days of creation in Genesis 1. In this case it suggests that Jesus is going to restore God's human creation, which was damaged by sin at the beginning. Or mention of the "third day" (2:1) may allude to God's manifesting himself at Sinai when he gave the law to Moses (Exodus 19:16), in which case it suggests that Jesus has come to reveal God's glory and to make a new covenant with humankind. Or both. Often John seems to intend more than one meaning.

At Cana, the fact that Jesus' mother is introduced even before Jesus underlines her significance. Nowhere else in biblical writings does a son address his mother as "Woman" (2:4). This unique manner of address connects Mary with another woman who was preeminently a mother: Eve, who is simply referred to as "woman" in Genesis 2:22–3:16 and "mother" in Genesis 3:20.

In effect, Jesus says to his mother (2:4), "That is your business. Why should I get involved?" In John's Gospel, Jesus characteristically puts off those who ask him for something (compare 4:47–48; 11:3–6). He operates on an agenda and schedule that cannot be determined or even known by anyone except his Father.

Mary seems to have no doubt that Jesus will, nevertheless, respond to her half-expressed request (2:5). Clearly she has faith in him. In the Gospel we watch the people around Jesus trying to discover who he is. Mary already knows him well enough to be confident of his power and his kindness. "Do whatever he tells you": her words sound in the ears of Jesus' disciples in every age. The attitude of this woman stands in contrast with that of the first woman, Eve, who did not do what God told her.

By transforming the water used for Jewish ritual purification, Jesus indicates that the Mosaic laws of ritual purity have served their purpose and are now surpassed by a more direct access to God. But the jars are not shattered as valueless; they are filled with something better—"a gift in place of a gift" (see 1:16). The Mosaic covenant is honored even as it is surpassed.

Jesus' miracle, which prolongs the wedding celebration, signals that the joyful time of God's intervention into human lives has arrived. Significantly, his first miracle is an act of transformation, promising transformation for ourselves.

Questions for Application

40 minutes
Choose questions according to your interest and time.

1 The disciples In this reading
   are very serious about seeking
   God. How serious a seeker of
   God are you? Have you given
   up seeking in frustration? Or
   are you too content to seek
   God? What might *you* have
   to leave behind if you were
   to become more serious about
   seeking God?

2 When Nathanael asks to know
   about Jesus, Philip says, "Come
   and see." What does it mean for
   a person to seek Jesus today?
   How do *you* seek Jesus? How
   might he be inviting you to take
   a step to "come and see" him?

3 Who has played the role of John
   the Baptist for you—pointing
   out Jesus to you? What can
   you learn from that person
   about how you might bear
   witness to others about Jesus?

4 How is it possible to know Jesus' titles but not grasp who he is? How has your understanding of him grown over time?

5 Mary does not give up when Jesus puts her off. When have you persisted in prayer? When have you given up? Where do you need to persist in prayer now?

"The leader must be careful not to talk too much. The traffic pattern of the group contribution should not be from leader to group member and then back to leader. Allow time for group discussion."

Gladys Hunt, *Gladys Hunt's "How-to" Handbook for Inductive Bible Study Leaders*

Approach to Prayer

15 minutes
Use this approach—or create your own!

♦ Read aloud this reflection
on Mary at Cana by Anthony
Bloom, an Orthodox bishop
in England.

As Mary, we too can make God's
kingdom come, wherever we
are . . . simply by having complete faith in the Lord. . . .
The fact that we are present in
a situation alters it profoundly
because God is then present with
us through our faith. Wherever
we are, at home with our family,
with friends . . . at work . . . we
can recollect ourselves and say,
"Lord, I believe in you, come and
be among us." . . . Sometimes
we have no words . . . but we can
always ask God to come and be
present. And we shall see how
often the atmosphere changes,
quarrels stop, peace comes.

Allow time for silent interces-
sory prayer, and let anyone
who wishes mention situations
where they want to see God
make his presence felt. End
by praying a Hail Mary and
an Our Father together.

A Living Tradition

St. Francis de Sales on Mary at Cana

This section is a supplement for individual reading.

The seventeenth-century bishop and writer St. Francis de Sales loved Scripture and quoted it so often that his contemporary, St. Vincent de Paul, referred to him as "a speaking Gospel." Here are a few of St. Francis's reflections on the wedding at Cana.

On Mary's request. The Blessed Virgin didn't make a long speech to present this couple's need to her divine Son. Skilled and knowledgeable in the art of praying well, she used the shortest but highest, best, and most efficient possible prayer. She said only these words: "My Son, they have no wine." By which she meant: "You're so kind and loving, and your heart is so compassionate and merciful. Please grant my request and do what I'm asking you for these poor people.". . .

What a very good prayer it is to simply present our needs to our Lord and then let him act, secure that he will see to them in the most beneficial way.

On Jesus' reply. "Woman, what concern is that to you and to me? My hour has not yet come." Certainly, at first, this answer seems quite harsh. That such a son would speak like this to such a mother! . . .

Really, this was a very loving answer. The Blessed Virgin understood its real meaning, and it made her feel like the most indulged mother of all time. Her heart remained filled with holy confidence, as shown in her words to the servants: "You heard what my son said, and because you don't understand love's language, you might think he refused me. Not at all! Don't be afraid. Just do whatever he tells you and don't worry. He will certainly meet your need."

On Mary's intercession. One last word about this Gospel passage: it teaches us that we should turn to Our Lady, since she has so much influence with her Son. And if we want her to present our needs to him, we must invite her to our banquet too. . . .

But notice that if we want Our Lady to ask her Son to change the water of our lukewarmness into the wine of his love, we must do whatever our Lord tells us. This is what the wine stewards did at Our Lady's directive. Let's imitate them. Let's fill our hearts with the water of repentance, and he will change this tepid water into the wine of fervent love.

Between Discussions

After the wedding celebration, Jesus leaves Cana for Capernaum, another town in Galilee, and then goes to Jerusalem for the Passover festival (2:13). There he performs a shocking symbolic act that contrasts sharply with the pleasant miracle at Cana. He enters the vast temple courtyard, makes a rope for himself (bringing weapons into the temple was forbidden), and drives out the merchants who are selling animals to be used in the sacrifices. Old Testament prophecies gave rise to the expectation that in the times of the Messiah the temple would be purified, perhaps even replaced (Zechariah 14:21; Jeremiah 7:11; Malachi 3:1; Isaiah 56:7). Against the background of these prophecies, Jesus would appear to be not only a religious person determined to put a stop to activities that profaned the holy place; he would also be seen as heralding the arrival of the messianic times. His action would have seemed that of a prophet, even of the Messiah.

John reports that "the Jews" challenge him to show his authorization (2:18). Here, as often in this Gospel, "the Jews" means specifically the religious leaders who refuse to accept Jesus' claims (the parallel accounts in the other Gospels refer to Jesus' challengers as "priests," "scribes," and "elders"—Matthew 21:23; Mark 11:27–28; Luke 20:1–2).

Jesus answers with a riddle (2:19). Like the parables that he often tells (reported in the other Gospels), his puzzling statements in John force his hearers to think and to acknowledge their own ignorance. Jesus seems to mean: "You are destroying the temple by your profanation, but I will raise up the new temple of the end times" (see Ezekiel 40–46). But there is an additional level of meaning: the end-times temple is to be Jesus himself, risen from the dead. The temple was the place where God made himself especially present to his people. Jesus himself will be this "place." He is the gift that replaces the earlier gift of the temple.

Zeal for the temple not only consumes Jesus in the sense of filling him with intense motivation (2:17); it eventually consumes him in the sense of destroying him, for his boldness in declaring his identity will provoke his opponents to put him to death.

John says that people in Jerusalem see Jesus' signs but do not grasp what the signs signify (2:23–25). He introduces as an example a man named Nicodemus (3:1–2). Jesus tells him that it is necessary to be born "again" or "from above" (3:3)—the Greek word means both. Jesus means both: being born "again," receiving a *new* life from God, and being born "from above," receiving a *heavenly* birth. Nicodemus is challenged to expand his understanding of God's action. So are we.

John has already told us that the Word has come down from heaven to reveal God. Now Jesus announces that he will return to heaven. He says he will be "lifted up" (3:14). The Aramaic word for lift up, which Jesus may have used, means both hang up (that is, crucify) and raise up (that is, exalt). Jesus' death will be agony and humiliation on a cross, but this will be part of Jesus' being raised up into the glory of God.

Jesus says that the Father "gave" the Son so the world might live (3:16). This implies that God gave the Son not only in his becoming a human being but in his laying down his life. God is not an angry deity needing to be appeased. The Father *gives* the Son, his most precious gift. He gives his Son not to allay his own anger but to conquer sin and evil for us, to overthrow the evil one, to release a flow of life-giving waters. What a generous Father! The Father is not like a wrathful monarch needing to be persuaded not to punish his rebellious subjects. He is like Abraham, grief-stricken at the prospect of his son's death but willing to give his beloved son for a higher purpose (Genesis 22). Significantly, earlier John spoke of Jesus in a way that likened him to Isaac: the father's "only son" (1:14) echoes Genesis 22:2, 12, 16.

In a final appearance, John the Baptist compares Jesus to a bridegroom (3:29). The incarnation of the Word is like a marriage, for in marriage each spouse enters fully into the other's life, agreeing henceforth to share the other's lot in life. Jesus inaugurated his public activity at Cana with a note of wedding joy. An allusion to a wedding will also be detectable in our next reading.

IF YOU KNEW WHO WAS ASKING YOU

Questions to Begin

15 minutes
Use a question or two to get warmed up for the reading.

1   What do you experience
     as the most difficult aspect
     of traveling? What aspect of
     traveling do you like best?

2   What is your least favorite
     household chore?

5 minutes
Read the passage aloud. Let individuals take turns reading
paragraphs.

The Reading: John 4:1–42

Revelation at the Well

[1] Now . . . [3] he left Judea and started back to Galilee. [4] But he had to go through Samaria. [5] So he came to a Samaritan city called Sychar. . . . [6] Jacob's well was there, and Jesus, tired out by his journey, was sitting by the well. It was about noon.

[7] A Samaritan woman came to draw water, and Jesus said to her, "Give me a drink." [8] (His disciples had gone to the city to buy food.)

[9] The Samaritan woman said to him, "How is it that you, a Jew, ask a drink of me, a woman of Samaria?" (Jews do not share things in common with Samaritans.)

[10] Jesus answered her, "If you knew the gift of God, and who it is that is saying to you, 'Give me a drink,' you would have asked him, and he would have given you living water."

[11] The woman said to him, "Sir, you have no bucket, and the well is deep. Where do you get that living water? [12] Are you greater than our ancestor Jacob, who gave us the well, and with his sons and his flocks drank from it?"

[13] Jesus said to her, "Everyone who drinks of this water will be thirsty again, [14] but those who drink of the water that I will give them will never be thirsty. The water that I will give will become in them a spring of water gushing up to eternal life."

[15] The woman said to him, "Sir, give me this water, so that I may never be thirsty or have to keep coming here to draw water."

[16] Jesus said to her, "Go, call your husband, and come back."

[17] The woman answered him, "I have no husband."

Jesus said to her, "You are right in saying, 'I have no husband'; [18] for you have had five husbands, and the one you have now is not your husband. What you have said is true!"

[19] The woman said to him, "Sir, I see that you are a prophet. [20] Our ancestors worshiped on this mountain, but you say that the place where people must worship is in Jerusalem."

[21] Jesus said to her, "Woman, believe me, the hour is coming when you will worship the Father neither on this mountain nor in Jerusalem. [22] You worship what you do not know; we worship what

we know, for salvation is from the Jews. 23 But the hour is coming, and is now here, when the true worshipers will worship the Father in spirit and truth, for the Father seeks such as these to worship him. 24 God is spirit, and those who worship him must worship in spirit and truth."

25 The woman said to him, "I know that Messiah is coming" (who is called Christ). "When he comes, he will proclaim all things to us."

26 Jesus said to her, "I am he, the one who is speaking to you."

Some Get It, Some Don't

27 Just then his disciples came. They were astonished that he was speaking with a woman, but no one said, "What do you want?" or, "Why are you speaking with her?" 28 Then the woman left her water jar and went back to the city. She said to the people, 29 "Come and see a man who told me everything I have ever done! He cannot be the Messiah, can he?" 30 They left the city and were on their way to him.

31 Meanwhile the disciples were urging him, "Rabbi, eat something."

32 But he said to them, "I have food to eat that you do not know about."

33 So the disciples said to one another, "Surely no one has brought him something to eat?"

34 Jesus said to them, "My food is to do the will of him who sent me and to complete his work. 35 Do you not say, 'Four months more, then comes the harvest'? But I tell you, look around you, and see how the fields are ripe for harvesting. 36 The reaper is already receiving wages and is gathering fruit for eternal life, so that sower and reaper may rejoice together. 37 For here the saying holds true, 'One sows and another reaps.' 38 I sent you to reap that for which you did not labor. Others have labored, and you have entered into their labor."

39 Many Samaritans from that city believed in him because of the woman's testimony, "He told me everything I have ever done." 40 So when the Samaritans came to him, they asked him to stay with them; and he stayed there two days. 41 And many more believed because of his word. 42 They said to the woman, "It is no longer because of what you said that we believe, for we have heard for ourselves, and we know that this is truly the Savior of the world."

10 minutes
Choose questions according to your interest and time.

1 What picture of the woman's personality do you get from this story?

2 What is it about Jesus that most impresses the woman? Why does it have such an impact?

3 Why does the woman leave her water jar (4:28)?

4 What exactly does Jesus want his disciples to see in verse 35? Consider verse 30.

5 What parallels can you find between Jesus' conversation with the woman (4:7–26) and his conversation with his disciples (4:31–38)?

A Guide to the Reading

If participants have not read this section already, read it aloud. Otherwise go on to "Questions for Application."

There were other ways to get from Judea to Galilee besides going through Samaria. Thus John's statement that Jesus "had" to go that way hints at a divine, rather than geographical, necessity. In God's providence, Jesus' conversation with the woman was not a random event but one that just had to happen—as some would say, a "divine appointment."

Cultural and religious barriers stood in the way of Jesus' speaking to the woman. Men did not converse with women in public, and Jews were not on friendly terms with Samaritans, whom they regarded as practicing an illegitimate form of Mosaic religion. But having bridged the infinite chasm between Creator and creation by becoming a human being, the divine Word was not going to let such lesser obstacles prevent him from talking to people.

Jesus strikes up a conversation with the woman by asking her for a drink. Apparently he is not put off by the ritual impurity (as Jews would see it) of her water jug (4:7). The woman's response is not necessarily friendly (4:9). In the view of one scholar, the woman "mocks Jesus for being so in need that he does not observe the proprieties." ("My, my, you really *must* be thirsty if you're asking *me* for a drink!")

Apparently Jesus is not put off by rudeness, either, for he turns the woman's response into an opportunity to discuss something more valuable than water (4:10). But the woman is thinking only about earthly realities (Jesus *has* caught her in the middle of her housework), and her response again has a mocking tone (4:11–12). She has a bucket and he doesn't, but now *he* is offering to get water for *her?*

Undeterred, Jesus explains that he is talking about heavenly water (4:13–14), that is, his teaching, his revelation of God, his gift of the Spirit. Given her previous remarks, we may wonder whether the woman's request (4:15) is sincere or sarcastic.

At this point Jesus brings the woman up short by showing that he knows about her private life (4:16–19; compare 1:47–49). Suddenly realizing that this Jewish traveler has some divine gift of insight, the woman opens a serious discussion with him about God's action in the world (4:20). Which is the true path to God:

Judaism, which is centered on the temple in Jerusalem, or Samaritanism, centered on the temple (destroyed long ago by the Jews) on nearby Mount Gerizim?

Jesus' answer again points to God's offer of a heavenly gift that surpasses earthly realities. God wishes to have—and through Jesus will soon have—men and women who worship him "in spirit and truth" (4:21–24). He does not mean worship with the inner spirit as opposed to external worship. The contrast is between worship in the earlier phase of God's activity, when the temple in Jerusalem was the locus of God's presence, and worship in the new phase, when the Spirit enables men and women to enter into heavenly worship. This is worship in response to the "truth" of God's revelation of himself in Jesus, the worship of God as "Father" by those who have become his children through Jesus (1:12). Worship centered on buildings is earthly and limited. Worship in the Spirit, which will be worship in the temple of Jesus' body (2:19–21), will be worship in a more intimate relationship with God.

The woman's response implies that she wonders whether her impressive prophetic visitor might be the Messiah, the end-times agent promised by God (4:25). Jesus acknowledges that he is the Messiah—and more. His answer could also be translated: "I AM is the one who is speaking to you." "I AM" is used as God's self-designation in Isaiah 43:10 and 45:18 (although this is not apparent in all translations).

When the disciples return, they are as "astonished" to see Jesus speaking with a woman as if they had seen a miracle (4:27; compare Luke 8:25). The following discussion shows that their thinking is just as earthbound as the woman's. Indeed, at that very moment the woman is setting an example of the missionary eagerness that Jesus is trying to convey to his disciples (4:29, 35).

There is subtle wedding symbolism in this episode. Repeatedly in the Old Testament we find scenes in which a man rests at a well, meets a woman, and a marriage is contracted or arranged (Genesis 24, 29; Exodus 2:15–21). At Sychar also a kind of marriage occurs—not an earthly wedding but a heavenly one, between the Lord and his people.

Questions for Application

40 minutes
Choose questions according to your interest and time.

1 Has a seemingly chance meeting ever played a part in your coming to know God more deeply?

2 Have you ever been uncomprehending when God tried to communicate with you, as the woman initially was unaware that God was breaking in on her ordinary routine?

3 What obstacles do you allow to prevent you from communicating God's word to the people around you?

4 Jews generally treated Samaritans as outcasts, but Jesus did not. How do you treat people who are different from you, especially fellow Christians who do not think as you do?

5 Reread 4:34. What food of this kind has God given you to nourish your life? Are you eating it?

6 How much room do your earthly goals and dreams leave for the life in the Spirit that God wishes to give you? How could you make a little more space?

7 How do you generally react when you hear about how God has acted in someone else's life? Does it build your faith, as it did for the Samaritan woman's neighbors? Does it stir up envy or hopelessness? What obstacles might stand in the way of your rejoicing at others' spiritual blessings? How could you remove these obstacles?

"Seek to ensure that every member contributes in one way or another. . . . If someone is doing too much talking, persuade that person to give others a chance."

Peter and Vita Toon, *Bible Study Starters*

Approach to Prayer

15 minutes
Use this approach—or create your own!

◆ Take a few minutes to recall that Jesus is as present in your group as he was to the Samaritan woman at the well. On behalf of the whole group, have someone ask Jesus for a drink of living water. "Lord, we thirst for you, for your word, your truth, your Holy Spirit. Let your living water gush up in us and out to others."

After a few minutes of silent reflection, end by praying together these lines from Psalms 63 and 42:

O God, you are my God,
  I seek you,
    my soul thirsts for you;
my flesh faints for you,
    as in a dry and weary land
      where there is no water.

As a deer longs for flowing
  streams,
    so my soul longs for you,
      O God.
My soul thirsts for God,
    for the living God.
When shall I come and behold
    the face of God?

Saints in the Making

Teresa of Avila on Living Water

This section is a supplement for individual reading.

St. Teresa of Avila, who lived in Spain in the sixteenth century, led a renewal of her religious congregation, the Carmelites, and is one of the Church's outstanding guides to prayer. Here are a couple of her responses to John's Gospel.

Oh, how many times do I recall the living water that the Lord told the Samaritan woman about! And so I am very fond of that Gospel passage. Thus it is, indeed, that from the time I was a little child, without understanding this good [thing] as I do now, I often begged the Lord to give me the water. I always carried with me a painting of this episode of the Lord at the well, with the words, inscribed: *Domine, da mihi aquam* [Lord, give me the water].

From *The Book of Her Life*

O compassionate and loving Lord of my soul! You likewise say: *Come to me all who thirst, for I will give you drink* [see John 7:37–38]. How can anyone who is burning in the living flames of cupidity for these miserable earthly things fail to experience great thirst? There is an extraordinary need for water so that one might not be completely consumed by this fire. I already know, my Lord, that out of Your goodness You will give it. You Yourself say so; Your words cannot fail. Well, if those accustomed to living in this fire and to being reared in it, no longer feel it or, like fools, do not succeed in recognizing their great need, what remedy is there, my God? You've come into the world as a remedy for needs such as these. Begin, Lord! Your compassion must be shown in the most difficult situations. Behold, my God, Your enemies are gaining a great deal. Have pity on those who have no pity on themselves; now that their misfortune has placed them in a state in which they don't want to come to You, come to them Yourself, my God. I beg this of You in their name; and I know that as they understand and turn within themselves and begin to taste You, these dead ones will rise.

From the *Soliloquies*

Between Discussions

How did the earliest Christians respond in prayer to the Gospel? One indication is contained in the New Testament writings, which quote and adapt the earliest Christian hymns. Probably the opening section of John's Gospel is adapted from a hymn used in the Christian communities that followed especially the tradition about Jesus that came from the Beloved Disciple—the tradition on which John's Gospel is based.

At the beginning of the twentieth century scholars discovered manuscripts of hymns which seem to have come from these communities associated with the Beloved Disciple and the Gospel of John. They are called the Odes of Solomon (for reasons that are not entirely clear). The forty-two odes are composed in Syriac, a dialect of the Aramaic language that Jesus and the apostles spoke. Thus the odes carry the flavor of worship in the early Aramaic-speaking, Jewish-Christian communities. The leading American scholar to have studied the odes, James H. Charlesworth, calls them the "first Christian hymnal." Charlesworth believes they were written at about the same time that the Gospel of John was being composed, probably between the years 90 and 100. Thus they make a fitting prayer accompaniment to the reading of John's Gospel. Here are three excerpts.

Ode 7 celebrates God's gentleness. He has concealed his majesty in order to show himself to us in a way that will not terrify us—by becoming one of us:

Joy over the Beloved brings in its fruits unhindered!
My joy is the Lord, my course leads toward him,
lovely is this path of mine.
    I have a helper, the Lord himself.
    In his sincere generosity he has let me know him,
    For his kindness diminished his grandeur.
He has become like me, so that I might resemble him;
he has appeared in my image, so that I might clothe myself with him.
    And I did not tremble when I saw him,
    because it is he himself who is gracious to me.
In nature he has become like me, so that I might join him.
In form he has become like me, so that I might not turn away from him.

Ode 30 calls the whole Church—the imperatives "fill" and "come" and "drink" are in the plural in the original language—to receive the living waters that Jesus promised during his earthly life and which he now makes available. The poet makes a subtle shift, from speaking of drinking from the waters of the Lord to speaking of drinking from the Lord himself. As in the previous ode, the poet marvels at the Incarnation, by which the unknowable God has "established himself" in our midst.

Fill yourselves with water from the living fountain of the Lord,
      because it has been opened for you.
Come, all you thirsty, drink
      and rest at the fountain of the Lord,
for it ripples with delight
      and refreshes the heart,
for its water is much sweeter than honey,
      and the honeycomb of bees cannot be compared to it,
for it issues forth from the lips of the Lord
      and from the Lord's heart flows out,
      and though it is limitless and invisible, it has come.

They did not know him until he established himself in their midst.
Blessed are they who have drunk from him
      and have rested in him. Alleluia.

In Ode 42 Jesus himself speaks, picking up the bridal imagery in the early chapters of John's Gospel (the marriage at Cana—2:1–11; John the Baptist's reference to Jesus as the bridegroom—3:29; the hint of betrothal in Jesus' relationship with the Samaritans—4) and combining it with the image of a yoke that he employs in Matthew 11:29–30.

Like the bridegroom's arm upon the bride,
      so is my yoke on those who know me.
And like the bridal couch spread out in the newlyweds' home,
      so is my love with those who trust me.

MY FATHER AND I

Questions to Begin

15 minutes
Use a question or two to get warmed up for the reading.

1 When you have been sick, whom have you relied on for help? Does anyone rely on you when they are sick?

2 What do you do or not do on Sunday to keep it as the Lord's Day?

5 minutes
*Read the passage aloud. Let individuals take turns reading
paragraphs.*

The Reading: John 5:1–30

A Poolside Healing Makes Waves

[1] After this there was a festival of the Jews, and Jesus went up to
Jerusalem. [2] Now in Jerusalem by the Sheep Gate there is a pool, called
in Hebrew Beth-zatha, which has five porticoes. [3] In these lay many
invalids—blind, lame, and paralyzed. [5] One man was there who had
been ill for thirty-eight years. [6] When Jesus saw him lying there and
knew that he had been there a long time, he said to him, "Do you
want to be made well?" [7] The sick man answered him, "Sir, I have no
one to put me into the pool when the water is stirred up; and while I
am making my way, someone else steps down ahead of me." [8] Jesus
said to him, "Stand up, take your mat and walk." [9] At once the man
was made well, and he took up his mat and began to walk.

Now that day was a sabbath. [10] So the Jews said to the man
who had been cured, "It is the sabbath; it is not lawful for you to
carry your mat." [11] But he answered them, "The man who made me
well said to me, 'Take up your mat and walk.'" [12] They asked him,
"Who is the man who said to you, 'Take it up and walk'?" [13] Now
the man who had been healed did not know who it was, for Jesus had
disappeared in the crowd that was there. [14] Later Jesus found him in
the temple and said to him, "See, you have been made well! Do not
sin any more, so that nothing worse happens to you." [15] The man
went away and told the Jews that it was Jesus who had made him
well. [16] Therefore the Jews started persecuting Jesus, because he was
doing such things on the sabbath. [17] But Jesus answered them, "My
Father is still working, and I also am working." [18] For this reason the
Jews were seeking all the more to kill him, because he was not only
breaking the sabbath, but was also calling God his own Father,
thereby making himself equal to God.

Like Father, Like Son

[19] Jesus said to them, "Very truly, I tell you, the Son can do nothing
on his own, but only what he sees the Father doing; for whatever the
Father does, the Son does likewise. [20] The Father loves the Son and
shows him all that he himself is doing; and he will show him greater
works than these, so that you will be astonished. [21] Indeed, just as the

51

Father raises the dead and gives them life, so also the Son gives life to whomever he wishes. 22 The Father judges no one but has given all judgment to the Son, 23 so that all may honor the Son just as they honor the Father. Anyone who does not honor the Son does not honor the Father who sent him. 24 Very truly, I tell you, anyone who hears my word and believes him who sent me has eternal life, and does not come under judgment, but has passed from death to life.

25 "Very truly, I tell you, the hour is coming, and is now here, when the dead will hear the voice of the Son of God, and those who hear will live. 26 For just as the Father has life in himself, so he has granted the Son also to have life in himself; 27 and he has given him authority to execute judgment, because he is the Son of Man. 28 Do not be astonished at this; for the hour is coming when all who are in their graves will hear his voice 29 and will come out—those who have done good, to the resurrection of life, and those who have done evil, to the resurrection of condemnation. 30 I can do nothing on my own. As I hear, I judge; and my judgment is just, because I seek to do not my own will but the will of him who sent me."

10 minutes
Choose questions according to your interest and time.

1 If Jesus knew so much about the man, why did he ask him whether he wanted to be healed (5:6)?

2 What reasons might Jesus have had for telling the man to carry his mat even though this violated the religious authorities' regulations for Sabbath rest?

3 Considering the information in verses 5 and 7, what might the man's life have been like after he was healed?

4 Docs Jesus' warning to the man to sin no more (5:14) necessarily imply that the man's sickness was caused by sin? (Consider 9:1–3.) If Jesus did not mean that the man's sickness was caused by sin, what other explanation might be given for what Jesus says in verse 14?

5 What three or four features of Jesus' relationship with his Father can you detect in this reading?

A Guide to the Reading

If participants have not read this section already, read it aloud. Otherwise go on to "Questions for Application."

John calls Jesus' miracles "signs" (2:11; 4:54) because he wishes us not simply to be amazed at them, but to ask what they mean.

Jesus' healing of a man who was sick for thirty-eight years signifies that he knows us and looks at us with compassion (5:6). Thomas Aquinas wrote, "Jesus saw him not only with his physical eyes, but also with the eyes of his mercy. This is the way David begged to be seen, saying: 'Look at me, O Lord, and have mercy on me' (Psalm 86:16)."

The deeper significance of the healing, however, emerges from the fact that Jesus chose to perform it on the Sabbath (5:9). From the number of cures that Jesus performed on the Sabbath (John 9:1–14; Mark 3:1–6), it seems that he may have deliberately provoked confrontations with the religious authorities as a way of bringing his unique relationship with God out into the open.

As Jesus must have foreseen, telling the healed man to carry away his mat (5:8) immediately upsets some of his fellow Jews (5:10–12—"the Jews" refers specifically to the religious authorities). Jesus defends himself by declaring that he is doing what his Father is doing (5:17). This enrages his listeners because, by calling God his Father and claiming to carry out God's work, Jesus has implied that he is on a par with God (5:18).

The point of contention is not how strictly the Sabbath should be kept or when exceptions should be made to the Sabbath rules. The issue is Jesus' identity. Jesus, in effect, says that he can dispense with the Sabbath rules because he is the fully authorized representative of the author of the Sabbath law. In Jewish culture, an agent was viewed as the complete representative of the sender. "A person's agent is as himself," it was said. An agent was empowered to say or do whatever was necessary to carry out the sender's commission. Within the scope of the commission, the agent was as if equal in authority to the sender. Often in business a father would send a son as his agent (the basis of Jesus' parable about himself in Mark 12:1–12). In our reading, Jesus presents himself as God's Son who acts as his Father's fully authorized agent in the world. (Having read the first verses of the Gospel, we know that Jesus is not an agent who acts *as if* he is equal to the one who sent him; he truly is on a par with the Father.) Jewish tradition recognized that while God rested on the Sabbath, there were nevertheless a couple of activities that he carried out on that day. Even on the Sabbath, babies are born and people die; so on the Sabbath God gives life and renders judgment. It is exactly these life-giving and judging functions that Jesus claims to exercise. Thus he is claiming divine prerogatives (Jesus speaks not about giving life to the newborn but giving life to the dead—5:21).

Jesus speaks of his life-giving and judging activities in both the present (5:21–25) and the future (5:28–29). Resurrection and judgment—events of the end times—have already begun through Jesus (5:25). Receiving Jesus' life now brings a resurrection from spiritual death that will culminate in resurrection from physical death. Believing in Jesus now means passing out of guilt and condemnation into peace with God—a passing through God's judgment that will ultimately be confirmed in the resurrection (5:29). Rejecting Jesus now means already experiencing judgment—a judgment that the disbeliever brings on himself or herself by rejecting the one who represents God.

The spiritual life that Jesus gives us now and the physical restoration of life that he will give in the future are two aspects of the same reality. One aspect brings us freedom from sin now; the other brings victory over death at the final resurrection. The life that Jesus gives now is eternal life; what he gives now is the first stage of the same life that will be given fully in the resurrection.

Questions for Application

40 minutes
Choose questions according to your interest and time.

1 In what area of your life—physical or otherwise—would you be the most surprised to experience healing? What might help you to keep on asking the Lord for his help?

2 Are you in a position to provide any kind of service to someone—in your family, neighborhood, local nursing home—who is struggling with a long-term affliction?

3 If Jesus truly is who he says he is in this reading—for example, in verse 24—how should you relate to him?

4 What does it mean to honor God (see 5:23)? What should you do to honor God?

5 Jesus exemplifies a human life lived in complete dependence on God (see especially 5:19, 30). How do you live in dependence on God? How might God be calling you to live in greater dependence on him?

6 Perhaps for private reflection rather than discussion: Think of a long-standing sin or weakness in your life. Have you considered that Jesus is well aware of this area of your life? How might his knowledge of you affect how you deal with this fault or weakness? How might it affect how you speak to him about it?

"A right response to Scripture is characterized by trust, obedience, praise, and thanksgiving. The application may include remembering an impressive truth, changing a wrong attitude, or taking a positive action."

The Navigator Bible Studies Handbook

Approach to Prayer

15 minutes
Use this approach—or create your own!

◆ Remembering the man who was sick for thirty-eight years, and bringing to mind your own long-term needs and those of others you know, pray Psalm 13 together.

How long, O Lord? Will you
     forget me forever?
          How long will you hide
               your face from me?
How long must I bear pain in
     my soul,
          and have sorrow in my
               heart all day long?
How long shall my enemy be
     exalted over me?
Consider and answer me,
     O Lord my God!
          Give light to my eyes,
               or I will sleep the sleep
               of death,
and my enemy will say, "I have
     prevailed";
          my foes will rejoice
               because I am shaken.
But I trusted in your steadfast
     love;
          my heart shall rejoice in
               your salvation.
I will sing to the Lord,
     because he has dealt
          bountifully with me.

End with a Glory to the Father.

Note: Next week's "Approach to Prayer" requires preparation.

A Living Tradition

Was He Patient—or Cranky?

This section is a supplement for individual reading.

How differently two readers can interpret the same passage! A case in point is the paralyzed man in this week's reading. Here are the views of an ancient and a modern commentator. Which do you find more persuasive? Why?

For thirty-eight years this man was paralyzed, and each year he watched others obtain health while he himself was bound by sickness. Yet he did not fall into despair, even though sadness for things past and complete hopelessness for things to come must have tortured him. . . . Learn how tragic was his situation. For when Christ asked him, "Do you want to be healed?" he answered, "Yes, Lord, but I don't have anyone to put me in the pool when the water is stirred." What words could be more pathetic? What situation could be more unfortunate? Do you see how his spirit had been subdued by the long years, his anger curbed and quieted? For he did not say anything blasphemous, as many do in calamities; he did not curse the day of his birth. He did not take offense at the question and say, "It is to ridicule and jeer at me that you ask whether I want to be healed?" No, very calmly and gently he answers, "Yes, Lord." And even though the man did not know who was questioning him—and had no idea that he was going to be healed by him—he mildly tells him everything and does not ask for anything at all, simply desiring to describe his situation. Perhaps he hoped Christ would help him by putting him into the water, and wished by these words to lead him to do so.
—St. John Chrysostom, 390

If the paralytic's malady were not so tragic, one could almost be amused by the man's unimaginative approach to the curative waters. His crotchety grumbling about the "whippersnappers" who outrace him to the water betrays a chronic inability to seize opportunity, a trait reflected again in his oblique response to Jesus' offer of a cure. The fact that he let his benefactor slip away without even asking his name is another instance of real dullness. Finally, he betrays his benefactor by reporting him to "the Jews." This is less an example of treachery . . . than of persistent naiveté.
—Raymond E. Brown, 1966

Between Discussions

The remainder of chapter 5 reports the continuation of the disagreement between the religious authorities and Jesus as a kind of judicial process. Jesus summons witnesses to his defense (5:31–40) and then makes countercharges against his adversaries (5:41–47). In effect he calls John the Baptist to the stand (5:33–35) and presents as evidence the remarkable works that he himself has been doing (5:36), the inner testimony of God in people's hearts (5:37–38), and the Old Testament Scriptures (5:39). All these testify to Jesus' authenticity.

It might be objected that Scripture warned against accepting anyone who presented himself as a prophet simply because he worked miracles (Deuteronomy 13:1–5). Furthermore, the manner in which the Old Testament writings pointed to Jesus was ambiguous enough that sincere people might reasonably disagree on the subject. Certainly Catholics take this view today in their religious conversations with Jews. But Jesus does not grant that failure to accept him might be based on well-intentioned misunderstanding. Quite the contrary. Why do those who sift the abundant evidence about him reach a negative conclusion? It is because something is amiss within their minds and hearts, he declares (5:42). They are more interested in fitting in to what other people think than seeking out what God thinks (5:44). They enjoy the honor they receive for being scrupulous observers of the Mosaic law according to the Pharisaic interpretation (5:42–44). Thus they read Scripture with a kind of blindness (5:45–47).

Jesus' diagnosis of the roots of his opponents' refusal to believe in him is not something we can transpose into our own situation. Unlike Jesus, who knew what was in people's hearts, we really do not know why people reach the decisions they do. We would be wrong to claim that bad motives lead people to refuse to acknowledge Jesus. We should also bear in mind that the people around us do not have the opportunity to see and hear Jesus directly, as did the residents of Jerusalem around the year 30. Today people see and hear Jesus only through his followers—and how clear a picture of him do they get from us?

We can, however, read Jesus' words as directed toward ourselves. When we are tempted to excuse the weakness of our faith, Jesus confronts us, as he confronted the religious leaders of his day. Has he not brought John the Baptists into our lives—people whose lives point us toward him? Has he not given us signs of his power and presence? Has he not revealed himself in our hearts? Has he not given us the testimony of Scripture and the teaching of the Church? How then can we rationalize our failures to trust him?

Centuries earlier, during the Israelites' years of wandering in the desert between Egypt and Canaan under the leadership of Moses, God had fed them miraculously with a breadlike food called manna. In Jewish tradition, the manna became an image of the wisdom of God, especially in his written word through Moses—the Law, Scripture. The manna also became an element in Jewish expectations of the end times: God would send the Messiah and open up the storehouses of heaven to feed his people with manna once again.

Against this background, Jesus multiplies bread and fish for thousands of people (6:1–15). As with the manna during the desert wandering, the people have enough to eat (6:11–13; Exodus 16:8, 12, 16, 18, 21). Is this, the crowds wonder, the manna of the end times? Is Jesus the Messiah? Yes, they conclude, and attempt to proclaim him king. They are partly right, but also partly, and very seriously, wrong, and Jesus flees from them.

There follows an incident in which Jesus makes his identity clearer to his disciples (6:16–21). During the night after the bread miracle, the disciples are out on the Sea of Galilee in a fishing boat. A storm comes up, and Jesus walks out to them across the surface of the waves. It is a moment of revelation. In the Old Testament, God is pictured as making his way across the sea, demonstrating his power over chaos and evil, and leading his people through the waters of the Reed Sea at the exodus from Egypt (Psalm 77:19). Jesus identifies himself with the name used by God in the Old Testament: "I am" (Exodus 3:14). While the crowds may view Jesus as a messiah bringing a kingdom of earthly blessings, his disciples at least should begin to perceive that he is much greater than that.

WHO EATS THIS BREAD WILL LIVE FOREVER

Questions to Begin

15 minutes
Use a question or two to get warmed up for the reading.

1   What was a very good sermon you have heard? What was so good about it?

2   What was a particularly painful gripe session that you have been in? Did you contribute to the complaining? How did the situation turn out?

The Reading: John 6:25–69

The Most Nourishing Food of All

25 They said to him, "Rabbi, when did you come here?" 26 Jesus
answered them, "Very truly, I tell you, you are looking for me, not because you saw signs, but because you ate your fill of the loaves. 27 Do
not work for the food that perishes, but for the food that endures for
eternal life, which the Son of Man will give you. For it is on him that
God the Father has set his seal." 28 Then they said to him, "What must
we do to perform the works of God?" 29 Jesus answered them, "This
is the work of God, that you believe in him whom he has sent."

30 So they said to him, "What sign are you going to give us
then, so that we may see it and believe you? What work are you per-
forming? 31 Our ancestors ate the manna in the wilderness; as it is
written, 'He gave them bread from heaven to eat.'" 32 Then Jesus said
to them, "Very truly, I tell you, it was not Moses who gave you the
bread from heaven, but it is my Father who gives you the true bread
from heaven. 33 For the bread of God is that which comes down from
heaven and gives life to the world." 34 They said to him, "Sir, give us
this bread always."

35 Jesus said to them, "I am the bread of life. Whoever comes
to me will never be hungry, and whoever believes in me will never be
thirsty. 36 But I said to you that you have seen me and yet do not believe. 37 Everything that the Father gives me will come to me, and anyone who comes to me I will never drive away; 38 for I have come down
from heaven, not to do my own will, but the will of him who sent me.
39 And this is the will of him who sent me, that I should lose nothing
of all that he has given me, but raise it up on the last day. 40 This is
indeed the will of my Father, that all who see the Son and believe in
him may have eternal life; and I will raise them up on the last day."

Take and Eat

41 Then the Jews began to complain about him because he said, "I am
the bread that came down from heaven." 42 They were saying, "Is not
this Jesus, the son of Joseph, whose father and mother we know? How
can he now say, 'I have come down from heaven'?" 43 Jesus answered
them, "Do not complain among yourselves. 44 No one can come to

me unless drawn by the Father who sent me; and I will raise that person up on the last day. 45 It is written in the prophets, 'And they shall all be taught by God.' Everyone who has heard and learned from the Father comes to me. 46 Not that anyone has seen the Father except the one who is from God; he has seen the Father. 47 Very truly, I tell you, whoever believes has eternal life. 48 I am the bread of life. 49 Your ancestors ate the manna in the wilderness, and they died. 50 This is the bread that comes down from heaven, so that one may eat of it and not die. 51 I am the living bread that came down from heaven. Whoever eats of this bread will live forever; and the bread that I will give for the life of the world is my flesh. . . .

53 "Very truly, I tell you, unless you eat the flesh of the Son of Man and drink his blood, you have no life in you. 54 Those who eat my flesh and drink my blood have eternal life, and I will raise them up on the last day; 55 for my flesh is true food and my blood is true drink. 56 Those who eat my flesh and drink my blood abide in me, and I in them. 57 Just as the living Father sent me, and I live because of the Father, so whoever eats me will live because of me. 58 This is the bread that came down from heaven, not like that which your ancestors ate, and they died. But the one who eats this bread will live forever."

Too Much to Swallow?

60 When many of his disciples heard it, they said, "This teaching is difficult; who can accept it?" . . . 66 Because of this many of his disciples turned back and no longer went about with him. 67 So Jesus asked the twelve, "Do you also wish to go away?" 68 Simon Peter answered him, "Lord, to whom can we go? You have the words of eternal life. 69 We have come to believe and know that you are the Holy One of God."

Questions for Careful Reading

10 minutes
Choose questions according to your interest and time.

1 How does the mood of Jesus' listeners change in the course of the reading?

2 What does it mean to "believe" in the one whom God has sent (6:29)? What do our readings thus far contribute to answering this question? What does this reading contribute? Cite specific statements in the text.

3 What are the similarities between what Jesus says in this reading and what he said in the reading in chapter 4? How does Jesus here go beyond what he said in chapter 4?

4 What role among "the twelve" does Peter play in verses 67 to 69?

"Be on the alert for the repetition of words, ideas, statements. This will often give you a clue as to the author's purpose."

Oletta Wald, *The Joy of Discovery*

A Guide to the Reading

If participants have not read this section already, read it aloud. Otherwise go on to "Questions for Application."

People question Jesus about when he came across the lake (6:25). The real question is *where* he came from. Jesus' origins are a mystery that the people have not grasped.

Jesus' speech, beginning at verse 32, has the form of a homily on a biblical text. The text, composed from various Old Testament passages, is proposed by his listeners: "He gave them bread from heaven to eat" (6:31). In verses 32 to 50 Jesus explores what the real "bread from heaven" is; in verses 51 to 58 he explains what it means to "eat" it.

Jews saw the manna as a symbol of God's law, God's wisdom (for example, see Deuteronomy 8:3). They regarded the Mosaic law, the Torah, as the real food that nourishes God's people—a food that they would "work" for (6:28) by studying and applying it to their lives. Jesus declares that the true heavenly bread is not the Torah but he himself. He is God's perfect food because he is God's perfect Word; to "work" at God's will is to grasp who he is and receive the life he has come to bring (6:29). Verse 33 could be translated "the bread of God is *he who* comes down from heaven."

Jesus is the Word of God—the truth and wisdom of God made visible, audible, and tangible. He is food because his truth and wisdom nourish our lives by revealing God to us and enabling us to journey toward God through earthly life.

Belief in Jesus is compared to eating: we receive him by taking him like food into our innermost being, accepting him as the source of our existence. To eat this food is to receive his revelation of God and act on it. Remember how Jesus said *his* food was *doing* the will of the one who sent him (4:34)?

When we receive Jesus, we receive God's perfect revelation of himself, for Jesus is the only one who has seen God (6:46) and has "come down" from heaven to reveal him (6:33, 38, 50). At the same time, Jesus is the one who has made a perfect human response to God (6:38). Receiving Jesus, then, we receive both God's love and the power to respond to his love.

When we are joined to God by knowing and responding to Jesus, God's life flows into us. We have life here (6:35) and hereafter (6:39–40). For those filled with God's life, death is no longer ultimate destruction but an entering more deeply into his presence (6:47–51).

At verse 51 Jesus sounds a new note. He will "give" his "flesh" "for the life of the world." This is sacrificial language. His gift of God's life will become available to us through his death for us.

Jesus goes on to speak differently about his followers eating the bread that he is (6:52–58). In Greek, he now uses a word for "eat" that means literally to crunch with the teeth (6:54, 56, 57, 58). Instead of speaking in terms of believing in him (as in 6:29, 47), Jesus speaks in terms of eating and drinking him. To believe in Jesus means making him the source of one's life, taking him into one's very being like food; to eat him involves believing in him, accepting him as the wisdom on which one builds one's life. The Word has become flesh (1:14). In the Eucharist, this flesh becomes our food.

Church Fathers saw Jesus' sermon as a declaration that he is the life-giving wisdom that reverses the effects of the false wisdom of rebellion against God that closed off the way to eternal life for human beings at the beginning of human existence. As punishment for sin, God drove the first couple away from the tree of life, lest they put forth their hands "and take also of the tree of life, and eat, and live forever" (Genesis 3:22). Now Jesus says, "Whoever eats of this bread, will live forever" (6:51). After man's sin, God "drove out the man" (Genesis 3:24). Jesus assures us that "Anyone who comes to me I will never drive away" (6:37). Gregory of Nyssa, a bishop of the fourth century, saw the eucharistic bread as the antidote for the poison of the forbidden fruit of sin.

Most of Jesus' followers are offended by this line of thinking (6:60–66). But Peter recognizes that no matter how cosmic are the claims that Jesus makes, he would be a fool to turn away from him. "Lord, to whom can we go?" (6:68). Disciples are those who remain with Jesus, even when they do not understand.

Questions for Application

40 minutes
Choose questions according to your interest and time.

1   What has been the underlying theme of your prayer and conversation with God over the last month or so? What does this tell you about your reasons for seeking God? What message do Jesus' words in verses 26 and 27 have for you?

2   Where in your journey through life—in work, family, home, difficult relationships, worries about money, children, etc.—do you most need to be nourished by the food that Jesus talks about in this reading? Are you coming to him for the food he wishes to give you?

3   Where is your greatest temptation to discouragement? What relevance does this reading have to this temptation? Which part of this reading is most helpful to you? Why?

√ 3 9

4 How can we help one another in the Church to receive the food that Jesus speaks about here? How about outside the Church as well?

5 Does your approach to communion line up with the realities set forth in this reading? What difference would it make if you were more consistently aware of Jesus' real presence in the Eucharist?

6 Are there areas of the teaching of Jesus and the Church that you struggle with? What does Peter's response to Jesus (6:68–69) suggest about how to handle this?

Approach to Prayer

15 minutes
Use this approach—or create your own!

♦ Before your meeting, designate
someone to obtain the words
and music for a couple of communion hymns that most of the
participants are familiar with.
Perhaps some used missalettes
may be obtained from the parish.
Sing these hymns together for
your prayer. End with an Our
Father, paying particular attention to the petition for "daily
bread." In the view of many
Church Fathers and modern
scholars, this petition is an
appeal for the food of the kingdom of God, thus, the Eucharist.

Saints in the Making

Real Food, Real Drink

This section is a supplement for individual reading.

In September 1979, Norman and Lita Poulin, of Winslow, Maine, celebrated their wedding anniversary by eating out at a nice restaurant. To Norman's great surprise, the evening's most memorable food—a teaching about "living bread" that would change and nourish his life—was yet to come.

Two or three people had told me about a priest who was in town giving some talks that weekend, Father John Bertolucci. I had seen his picture in the paper but hadn't paid too much attention till my daughter-in-law told me, "You ought to go hear him. You'd like it." I remembered that as Lita and I left the restaurant. "Why don't we go see what's going on?" I suggested.

Father Bertolucci turned out to be a dynamic speaker, and his whole talk had me on the edge of my seat. But what especially touched me was his explanation of the part of John's Gospel where Jesus says "I am the bread of life. . . . My flesh is true food and my blood is true drink" (6:48, 55). I had never really thought much about that, though I considered myself a normal Catholic. I went to church on Sundays, received Communion, prayed my rosary, did my daily prayers. But I didn't have a deep relationship with the Lord and had forgotten what the Eucharist really is.

That night was a turning point. Right away, I looked up that passage, started reading the Gospel of John, and fell in love with it. I took a Scripture course from our parish priest and began studying the Bible. At Father Bertolucci's suggestion, I dropped in on a charismatic prayer group—*Amor Dei,* which meets in my own parish of St. John the Baptist—and have been a member ever since. Personal prayer became a deep joy—so much so that I forgot about hunting and fishing on my trips up into the wilderness country and spent the time praying and admiring the beauty of God's creation!

The Eucharist means a lot to me now. I think more about what a privilege it is to have Jesus come to me as real food and drink. That's why I always ask the Blessed Mother to help me receive his body and blood in the right manner, with the right attitude.

Between Discussions

In the time of Jesus, the physical and spiritual center of Judaism
was the temple in Jerusalem. The temple complex was one of
the most impressive sites in the early first-century world. While
the temple building itself was small, it was surrounded by vast
courtyards, covering more than thirty acres, enclosed by majestic
porticoes and entered by grand stairways. Here was space to accommodate the hundreds of thousands of visitors who crowded
into Jerusalem three times a year for the pilgrimage festivals. Here
God dwelled among his people in a special way.

After the miracle of bread (chapter 6), Jesus takes his
teaching ministry right into the temple. There, in the midst of one
of the great pilgrimage feasts, he announces that God's life-giving
power is now available in him (chapters 7–8).

Jesus uses the particular festival being celebrated to am-
plify his message. The festival is called "Booths," or "Tabernacles."
This autumn festival occurs when farmers in Israel are looking
forward to the winter rains. Thus it contained ceremonies asking
God to send abundant rains. The feast took its name from the
"booths," or leafy huts, that pilgrims built for themselves for the
eight days of the festival, recalling the Israelites' tents when they
traveled through the Sinai desert from Egypt to Canaan. This
historical dimension of the feast also brought water to mind, for
God had miraculously provided water for the desert travelers
(Numbers 20:1–13; Psalm 78:16). In addition, the feast looked
forward to the end times, when God would send the Messiah and
make his people holy. Here too water was involved, for the
prophets used the image of water gushing out of the temple and
flowing out of Jerusalem to represent God's end-times presence
among his people (Ezekiel 47:1–12; Zechariah 14:8).

Imagine the effect when Jesus stands up to declare that
he is the source of living water (7:37–39)! *He* is the answer to all
prayers for life-giving rain. The water in the desert was an image of
the life of God that *he* now brings. He, the new temple, is the source
of waters that Ezekiel and Zechariah had foreseen.

Along with water, the feast of Booths involved the symbolism of light. The feast recalled the pillar of fire by which God

accompanied the Israelites in the desert (Exodus 13:21). The feast looked forward to the continuous day of the messianic age (Zechariah 14:7). At night, huge lamp stands were set up in the temple courtyard, and the men danced by their light. At the end of the festival, Jesus declares to the crowd, "I am the light of the world" (8:12). He is the revelation of God, the light that transforms people's lives. His light shines more brightly than the light of the Mosaic law, as the sun outshines street lamps at noon.

Throughout these chapters Jesus responds to objections (7:21–24; 8:17–18) and makes counteraccusations (7:19; 8:19, 37–47). The question of Jesus' origin arises: people think they know where he comes from (7:27–28, 41–42), but since they do not recognize that he has come from God (1:1–3), they are really in the dark about him (8:14).

Jesus repeatedly affirms that he is God's agent (7:16–18, 29; 8:16, 26, 28–29, 42, 55) and again he identifies himself with God (8:24). He declares that spiritual and moral freedom comes from abiding in his word; indeed, the one who keeps his word will not experience death (8:31–32, 36, 51). Before Abraham was, Jesus declares, "I am" (8:58). Such extraordinary claims provoke Jesus' listeners to hurl accusations (and try to hurl stones) at him (7:20; 8:48, 52, 59). Meanwhile the religious authorities begin to attempt to eliminate him (7:32, 44). But the crowds and even the temple officials are divided in their estimate of him (7:12, 15, 25–27, 40–43, 45–51; 8:30).

As evidence for his claim to be God's light, Jesus gives sight to a blind man (chapter 9). But because he does so in a way that breaks the regulations for the Sabbath rest promoted by some of the religious leaders, the healing brings him into renewed conflict with them. The blind man, who at first does not know who Jesus is, acknowledges his ignorance and is willing to learn. Thus he becomes able to see in more than one sense. Those who reject Jesus insist that they do know him. While in a physical sense they see, in a spiritual sense they have made themselves blind. Jesus' response to these spiritually blind leaders constitutes our next reading.

My Sheep Hear My Voice

Questions to Begin

15 minutes
Use a question or two to get warmed up for the reading.

1 Do you like to take care of animals? Why or why not?

2 How good are you at recognizing people on the phone simply by the sound of their voice?

5 minutes
Read the passage aloud. Let individuals take turns reading
paragraphs.

The Reading: John 10:1–33

Job Description of the Finest Shepherd

1 "Very truly, I tell you, anyone who does not enter the sheepfold by the gate but climbs in by another way is a thief and a bandit. 2 The one who enters by the gate is the shepherd of the sheep. 3 The gate-keeper opens the gate for him, and the sheep hear his voice. He calls his own sheep by name and leads them out. 4 When he has brought out all his own, he goes ahead of them, and the sheep follow him because they know his voice. 5 They will not follow a stranger, but they will run from him because they do not know the voice of strangers." 6 Jesus used this figure of speech with them, but they did not understand what he was saying to them.

7 So again Jesus said to them, "Very truly, I tell you, I am the gate for the sheep. 8 All who came before me are thieves and bandits; but the sheep did not listen to them. 9 I am the gate. Whoever enters by me will be saved, and will come in and go out and find pasture. 10 The thief comes only to steal and kill and destroy. I came that they may have life, and have it abundantly.

11 "I am the good shepherd. The good shepherd lays down his life for the sheep. 12 The hired hand, who is not the shepherd and does not own the sheep, sees the wolf coming and leaves the sheep and runs away—and the wolf snatches them and scatters them. 13 The hired hand runs away because a hired hand does not care for the sheep. 14 I am the good shepherd. I know my own and my own know me, 15 just as the Father knows me and I know the Father. And I lay down my life for the sheep. 16 I have other sheep that do not belong to this fold. I must bring them also, and they will listen to my voice. So there will be one flock, one shepherd. 17 For this reason the Father loves me, because I lay down my life in order to take it up again. 18 No one takes it from me, but I lay it down of my own accord. I have power to lay it down, and I have power to take it up again. I have received this command from my Father."

19 Again the Jews were divided because of these words. 20 Many of them were saying, "He has a demon and is out of his mind. Why listen to him?" 21 Others were saying, "These are not the words of one who has a demon. Can a demon open the eyes of the blind?"

If Today You Hear His Voice . . .

22 At that time the festival of the Dedication took place in Jerusalem. It was winter, 23 and Jesus was walking in the temple, in the portico of Solomon. 24 So the Jews gathered around him and said to him, "How long will you keep us in suspense? If you are the Messiah, tell us plainly." 25 Jesus answered, "I have told you, and you do not believe. The works that I do in my Father's name testify to me; 26 but you do not believe, because you do not belong to my sheep. 27 My sheep hear my voice. I know them, and they follow me. 28 I give them eternal life, and they will never perish. No one will snatch them out of my hand. 29 What my Father has given me is greater than all else, and no one can snatch it out of the Father's hand. 30 The Father and I are one."

31 The Jews took up stones again to stone him. 32 Jesus replied, "I have shown you many good works from the Father. For which of these are you going to stone me?" 33 The Jews answered, "It is not for a good work that we are going to stone you, but for blasphemy, because you, though only a human being, are making yourself God."

10 minutes
Choose questions according to your interest and time.

1 What are the characteristics of the kind of leadership that Jesus claims to exercise in this reading? Cite specific statements in the text.

2 What does the good shepherd gain from his relationship with the sheep? What do the sheep gain from their relationship with him?

3 What kind of response does the good shepherd seek from his sheep?

4 In verses 1 to 15 Jesus contrasts himself with the religious authorities. What are his criticisms of them? What is their criticism of him?

5 Read Ezekiel 34:1–16, a prophecy with which Jesus and the Jewish leaders would have been familiar. What does this passage contribute to your understanding of the good-shepherd image?

A Guide to the Reading

If participants have not read this section already, read it aloud. Otherwise go on to "Questions for Application."

Jesus does not present a unified parable in verses 1 to 18. Rather, shepherding supplies various images—sheep, shepherd, sheepfold—that enable him to make a number of points. It is better not to try to picture Jesus as both gate (10:7) and shepherd (10:11) simultaneously.

In the ancient Near East, *shepherd* was a metaphor for *king*. Through shepherding imagery, then, Jesus contrasts two systems of leadership. The first is that of the religious authorities, to whom he is speaking (10:6). They are angry at him for breaking the Sabbath rest by the way he healed a blind man (9:13–16; notice the reference in 10:21). Jesus asserts that they lead God's people only in order to benefit themselves: like sheep-stealers, they seize the sheep, presumably either to sell them for a profit or to eat them (10:1, 10); like hired hands, they tend them only for wages, not out of love (10:12–13). Later Jewish sources would express severe criticism of the corrupt and violent practices of some of the religious authorities in Jesus' day.

But Jesus is not calling for a mere reformation of the religious authorities, just as his clearing of the temple was not merely a protest against unjust economic practices (2:13–22). He presents himself as the leader who will replace the existing leaders of God's people. He is *the* shepherd, *the* rightful leader of God's people (10:11). He will exercise a radically better kind of leadership because the sheep—men and women—*belong* to him (10:14). Only one who is divine could make this claim.

From early in the Gospel—two years earlier, in John's account—Jesus has been dropping hints that he is going to die in a way that will benefit others. He announced that he would be raised up like the bronze figure of a snake that God used to bring healing to the Israelites centuries earlier in the wilderness (3:14); that he would give his flesh for the life of the world (6:51). Now Jesus states more clearly than before that he intends to relinquish his life (10:15). The Father is completely generous to the Son: all that the Father has, he gives to the Son (3:35). Now Jesus will be completely generous with his followers: he will give them his life (10:15).

Thus, rather than causing him to exercise a more severe rule over people, Jesus' right of ownership causes him to lead them in a way that is totally geared to *their* good. How contrary to worldly expectations! Jesus' analogy of the shepherd who lays down his life for his sheep only brings out the astonishing unexpectedness of his approach to leadership, for why would any shepherd, whether owner or not, actually die to save his sheep?

While this kind of leadership seems completely contrary to human expectations, human beings instinctively recognize it as the leadership they desire. Learning of Jesus' self-sacrificing love, men and women will say, "Ah, at last, *this* is the leader I have been waiting for" (see 10:4–5, 11–16).

Jesus is shepherd of a large flock (10:16), but he knows each sheep individually (10:14)—like the mother of a large family, whose heart is big enough to love each child as though he or she were her only one. Each sheep will hear his or her individual name called by the shepherd. Each will hear the shepherd saying, "For *you* I have laid down my life and have taken it up again."

Jesus speaks of overlapping relationships of knowledge and love. The Father knows Jesus; Jesus knows his followers (10:14–15). From eternity the Son has been with God in the intimacy of perfect knowledge and love (see 1:1–3). Now Jesus will draw men and women into this eternal knowing-and-being-known between Father and Son.

The dialogue in verses 22 through 33 takes place at the feast of the dedication of the temple (10:22). The feast celebrated the consecration of the altar after it was profaned during the persecution of the Jews by the Syrian emperor Antiochus Epiphanes IV. Jesus presents himself as the new temple, the new altar, the locus of the new sacrifice that will bring God's life to men and women (just after our target reading—at 10:36—he refers to his being "sanctified," set apart for holy use, by the Father).

Jesus' opponents are right about the meaning of his words (10:33, referring to 10:30), but they are wrong about whether his words are true. Jesus is not "making" himself God, as his opponents say. He *is* God (1:1–3).

Questions for Application

40 minutes
Choose questions according to your interest and time.

1   When have you become aware that God has called you before you called to him—that he gave you the grace to seek him? How might the recollection of this experience affect your relationship with him today?

2   Sheep are easily led and help-less creatures. What might Jesus be implying about us in our relationship to him by referring to us as his sheep? How should this affect how you relate to him?

3   Through whom have you heard the voice of the good shepherd?

4   Describe a situation in which you faced the challenge of laying down your life in some fashion. How did you change through this experience? What did you learn from it?

5   How much effort do you invest in getting to know your fellow parishioners by name? your neighbors? the people you work with? How could you grow in taking a personal interest in them?

6 What could you do to become more alert to the Lord's voice in your life?

7 Look back to question 5 on page 17. Have your questions been answered as you have read further in John? What unanswered questions do you have as you complete the readings from John in this booklet? How will you pursue these questions?

"The purpose of group Bible study is to better understand God's word in order to live it—not to have intellectual or emotional mastery of it."

Rena Duff, *Sharing God's Word Today*

Approach to Prayer

15 minutes
Use this approach—or create your own!

◆ In his letter to the Romans, St. Paul spoke about God's love for us through Jesus in a way that sounds almost like a homily on John 10:28. Have someone read Romans 8:31–39 aloud. Allow a few minutes for participants to offer short prayers of thanks to God for his love. Close with a Hail Mary and an Our Father.

A Living Tradition

Be on the Lookout for Him

This section is a supplement for individual reading.

From a sermon by Cardinal John Henry Newman, a nineteenth-century English theologian.

He is our shepherd, and "the sheep know his voice." If we are his sheep, we shall hear it, recognize it, and obey it. Let us beware of not following when he goes before: "He goes before, and his sheep follow him, for they know his voice." Let us beware of receiving his grace in vain. When God called Samuel, he answered, "Speak, Lord, for thy servant heareth." When Christ called St. Paul, he "was not disobedient to the heavenly vision." Let us desire to know his voice; let us pray for the gift of watchful ears and a willing heart. He does not call all men in one way; he calls us each in his own way. To St. Peter he said, "Follow thou me"; of St. John, "If I will that he tarry till I come, what is that to thee?"

Nor is it always easy to know his voice. St. John knew it, and said, "It is the Lord," before St. Peter. Samuel did not know it till Eli told him. St. Paul asked, "Who art thou, Lord?" We are bid, "try the spirits, whether they be of God." But whatever difficulty there be in knowing when Christ calls, and whither, yet at least let us look out for his call.

Let us not be content with ourselves; let us not make our own hearts our home, or this world our home, or our friends our home; let us look out for a better country, that is, a heavenly. Let us look out for him who alone can guide us to that better country; let us call heaven our home, and this life a pilgrimage; let us view ourselves, as sheep in the trackless desert, who, unless they follow the shepherd, will be sure to lose themselves, sure to fall in with the wolf.

We are safe while we keep close to him.

After Words

If all we knew of Jesus' life was the portion covered by John in the part of the Gospel we have been reading, our knowledge of him would be incomplete. We would know that he is a divine person, the Word of God, while being also fully human. We would know, therefore, that he is in a position to reveal God; that he can exercise God's power to give life, even to overcome death. This, by itself, would be of immense significance for us. We would indeed have a great deal to ponder about him and our relationship with him. Yet there would remain much about Jesus that we would not understand. For his revelation of God consists not only in his becoming a human being, which shows that God is humble and generous beyond imagining. It consists not only in his signs, which show that God is both compassionate and powerfully present among us. The full revelation of God that Jesus brings appears in the *whole* life that he lives and the death that he accepts. In fact, the revelation of God in Jesus involves even more than this, for it includes his resurrection. Only when we see Jesus' life and death, and know him as risen, do we get the full picture of God that Jesus provides—a God who loves us with complete self-giving, and whose self-giving is so powerful that it overcomes death.

If we had only the first ten chapters of John's Gospel, we would, in fact, be in danger of forming a distorted picture of Jesus. We might see him as an immensely powerful figure who can transform and multiply elements of the material world at will; who can restore people's bodies to health; and who grants people a share in God's life—all without much effort on his part. Aside from ordinary tiredness and thirst, and, we might infer, ordinary annoyance at the obtuseness and hostility of the people he has to deal with, Jesus does not seem to suffer in the episodes of the Gospel that we have just read. He travels around, dispensing spectacular favors to people, mostly on his own initiative. He might almost seem like a kind of superman. It is true that he hints obscurely that he will suffer a violent death. But if we were to evaluate him on the basis of the first ten chapters alone, we might be in danger of agreeing with the conclusion reached by many of the people who witnessed his multiplication of bread and fish. "Here indeed is

God's supreme agent, come to bring us a wonderful life in this world. Let us welcome him and take him as our leader. Even if we do not fully understand him, we can be sure he will make our lives easier and happier." Jesus fled from the people who had this misunderstanding of him.

Our reading has brought us only halfway through John's account of Jesus. We need to read on to the end to get the whole picture. Only when we see Jesus' suffering and dying do we glimpse the depths of divine love that Jesus has come to reveal. At the cross we see the Father giving his Son generously for the life of the world, and we see the Son giving himself generously to the Father for the life of the world. The cross reveals that God is not a solitary potentate residing in bliss at an infinite distance from humankind; rather he is a Father and a Son whose limitless love for one another spills over in self-giving for the human race.

The part of John's Gospel that we have read so far shows us the Word of God "coming down" into our world to bring us God's life. The remainder of the Gospel shows us Jesus going back "up" to God—first on the cross, then in resurrection from the dead and ascension to God's presence. It does not take long to read through the rest of John's Gospel. In my version of the Bible, it is only another thirteen pages. Why not read on and get the whole picture?

If you have found this booklet helpful, you may be interested in the sequel—*John 11–21: My Peace I Give You.*

A Backward Glance

Finding and Reflecting on the Larger Themes in John 1 through 10

Picasso's massive painting *Guernica* stands twelve feet high and extends more than twenty-five feet in width. The viewer has to be at a considerable distance from such an immense work to take it all in. The exhibition hall in the Madrid museum where *Guernica* hangs allows the visitor to stand back far enough to see the entire picture in a single view. Only at a distance can the viewer feel the full impact of the painting.

A similar standing back at a distance is required to appreciate the Gospel of John. John's Gospel is not the longest book in the Bible, but it tells the largest story, for it begins before time began and looks forward to the resurrection at the end of time. No other biblical book has such an immense sweep. In the present booklet we have examined only the first half of John's Gospel—the left side of his extensive canvas, so to speak. Hopefully you will go on to read the rest of the Gospel. But before you do, now is a good moment to stand back and consider what you have read so far, in order to notice the larger features and ask what meaning they may have for you.

Here are a few observations about larger themes in John's Gospel and lines of personal reflection that they suggest.

Word, truth, light. As we have seen, John portrays Jesus as God's Word coming into the world, bringing the light of eternal life for men and women. As God's Word, Jesus reveals God perfectly, for he truly knows God. This is why Jesus declares that he is the truth (14:6): he means that he perfectly reveals God, God's plans, God's way of life. In the background of this portrayal of Jesus is the Old Testament image of Lady Wisdom coming among people, offering her riches to any who will accept her invitation. Like Lady Wisdom, Jesus meets with a mixed response: some accept him, many reject him.

Our own response to Jesus may hinge on whether we experience a need for wisdom. If we feel that we have our lives pretty much under control and moving in the right direction, our motivation to seek wisdom may be weak. On the other hand, if we feel that we are making a mess of our lives, we are likely to be more interested in an offer of wisdom. This is why people whose

lives are in crisis are sometimes more open to a radical conversion
to God.

Most people are probably somewhere between these ex-
tremes. We do not harbor the illusion that we are in control of our
lives. But our lives are not in crisis, either—at least most of the
time. Some things in our lives are settled; some aren't. We may not
fully recognize how greatly we need God's grace, yet we are em-
barking on Bible study because we are eager to find some wisdom.

Perhaps our sense of need for God might be sharpened by
thinking back on past experiences where our lack of wisdom became apparent. Many of us remember with regret how we wasted
some opportunities in our youth or hurt people close to us as we
made the transition from childhood to adulthood. In retrospect, we
may realize that we entered marriage without being quite ready for
the responsibilities. We may sadly admit that we have sometimes
failed to respect or appreciate or support our spouse. Most of us
who are parents are aware of our mistakes in raising our children
(we were too demanding, demanding about the wrong things, not
demanding enough . . .).

For myself, such recollections illustrate my ability to proceed confidently in the wrong direction. And there is no reason for
me to think that the person who blindly made the mistakes that I
made in the past might not make other mistakes in the future.
Indeed, it rather seems likely that I am at present making mistakes
which I do not yet perceive. This helps me realize that my need for
God's wisdom is probably greater than I am conscious of—which is
a good frame of mind for reading John's Gospel.

Beyond earthbound thinking. The woman who thinks
that Jesus is offering her well-water (4:11) and the people who
think that Jesus has come to run a miraculous bakery (6:14–15)
are operating with a this-world-only kind of thinking that prevents
them from understanding Jesus' heavenly origin and the heavenly
life that he offers. We can view these people as our representatives. Don't we too, by and large, tend to have an earthbound
vision of our lives? Don't we tend to invest ourselves in planning
just for earthly life? Don't we tend to value what society considers

valuable rather than what God considers valuable? Don't we, like many of the people in John's Gospel, tend to judge by appearances, rather than penetrating to reality as God sees it (see 7:24)? Jesus tells the crowd who listens to him, "I am from above; you are of this world" (8:23). That's us, all right!

Reading the Gospel of John confronts us with a choice. Will we remain enclosed in our earth-only perspective that is resistant to God's wisdom? Or will we take hold of Jesus' revelation of God? If we do, he will gradually free us from this-worldly thinking. "If you continue in my word, you are truly my disciples; and you will know the truth, and the truth will make you free" (8:31–32). If we prefer the values of the world around us (see 5:44; 12:43) and are reluctant to let go of our sins (see 3:19–20), we can at least ask God for the grace to open ourselves to the transformation of our thinking that he wishes to work in us.

The saints are a help here. They constantly direct our attention to God and the life that lies beyond our present life. This makes them challenging, even discomfiting. And the saints show that the offer Jesus makes in John 8:32 is real. It *is* possible to have one's mind and heart transformed by God's grace, so that one's life is directed toward God and his kingdom. The saints got free from earthbound thinking by becoming focused on God's love.

The centrality of Jesus. Unlike the other three Gospels, John's Gospel, especially the first ten chapters, does not tell us a great deal about how to live as followers of Jesus. Most of what Jesus says on this subject in John's Gospel is gathered into his conversation with his disciples at the Last Supper (chapters 13–16). In the earlier chapters, John focuses on the fundamental issue: Who is this Jesus that we are to follow?

Jesus' statement to the woman he meets at the well expresses this focus. "If you knew the gift of God, and who it is that is saying to you, 'Give me a drink,' you would have asked him, and he would have given you living water" (4:10). Who *is* Jesus? What *does* he offer us? What does it mean to receive what he offers? These are the questions that John constantly challenges us to explore. John shows people meeting Jesus and being challenged by him to come to full faith in him. These incidents spur us to ask, What *is* full faith in Jesus? How does Jesus challenge *me* to grow in faith in him?

Of course, in one sense, if we are Christians, we already have the answers. We know Jesus is the Word of God, God's Son, Christ, the Lord. Yet John must have thought that it was important for Christians to ponder anew the basic questions about Jesus' identity and the life he offers, for John wrote his Gospel mainly for Christians. His readers had already entered a relationship with Jesus. They believed in him. Yet John describes one episode after another in which people who meet Jesus wrestle with the question of who he is. In many cases, John highlights the stages of their progress toward full faith in him. Apparently John thought that the process of coming to full faith in Jesus was valuable for the members of his church to reflect on. In one sense, they had already come to full faith in Jesus. In another sense, they had not yet fully comprehended who Jesus is.

We are probably not very different from John's first readers. We are familiar with the correct terminology about Jesus, but are our minds shaped by this knowledge? We are familiar with Jesus' heavenly origin and destiny; but how deep an impact has he made on our lives? Reading the Gospel of John, I am spurred to ask whether Jesus is the living center of my life. Is it my first priority to go through each situation today in union with him, who is the light and the truth?

A Sentence Can Speak Volumes

On the one hand, John's Gospel has a grand pattern—the Word comes into the world as a human being, reveals God, and by way of cross and resurrection returns to God—and it is crucial to keep the pattern in view as we read each part of John's account. On the other hand, John writes in a way that invites us to pause at almost every sentence and probe into its depths. Thus at times it is the whole plan of salvation that impresses us: the Word became a human being for *me!* At other times, we may be struck by a single statement, even by a single word.

The first time I read John's Gospel all the way through, one sentence had a special impact on me. To explain the experience, I need to give you a little background.

I drifted away from my Catholic upbringing during high school. In college I reached the conclusion that there is no God. Nevertheless I could not lay the question of God to rest. I read and talked about religion, and even took college courses on various religions. Then I met someone who suggested I read the Gospel of John.

I read through the first couple of chapters without finding anything that answered any of my questions. Then, at the end of chapter 2, a statement of John's caught my attention. "Many believed in his name when they saw the signs that he gave, but Jesus knew them all and did not trust himself to them; he never needed evidence about any man; he could tell what a man had in him" (2:23–25). I am quoting from the Jerusalem Bible translation, because that is the one I was reading at the time. In fact I can see the heavy, four-inch-thick volume opened before me on the mustard-colored carpet where I was sprawled out reading, as clearly as though it were yesterday, although it was more than thirty years ago.

John's remark had the flavor of a personal observation. John had evidently spent time with Jesus and had gotten to know him. He had watched Jesus draw on some hidden source of insight into people's minds and hearts. From these observations John had grown to admire Jesus, to love him. He was writing about Jesus out of this personal familiarity.

As I pondered this, I thought about the personal knowledge and love of Jesus, which his disciples had gained, being passed on by them to other people. By the disciples' words, people who had never met Jesus in the flesh experienced his presence. They too came to know Jesus and to love him. Mentally I followed this line of people through time, from the first century to the twentieth century. That is what still happens today, I realized. In some mysterious way, people who already know and love Jesus communicate their knowledge of him to other people, and those people themselves then come to know him as a real, living person. *Why,* I thought with a start, *that could happen to me!* I too could enter into this knowledge of Jesus that countless other people have shared.

Over the following days and weeks, I continued to think about the possibility of knowing Jesus that the passage in John had helped me perceive. It helped me take some steps in faith that soon brought me back to Christ and into the life of the Church.

Looking back, it seems a curious experience. The statement in John's Gospel about Jesus' knowledge of people's hearts is hardly one of his central proclamations of Jesus' identity. John's remark is little more than an aside. And the reflections it stirred in me went beyond the message that John was communicating. Yet that was the passage that started me thinking. God made my reading it a grace-filled opportunity to get past a barrier that lay in the way of my believing in him.

I offer my experience to you as an encouragement to read John's Gospel slowly and prayerfully. Who knows what sentence, what word, might be an opportunity of grace for you?

Suggestions for Bible Discussion Groups

L ike a camping trip, a Bible discussion group works best if you agree on where you're going and how you intend to get there. Many groups use their first meeting to talk over such questions. Here is a checklist of issues, with bits of advice from people with experience in Bible discussions. (A planning discussion will go more smoothly if the leaders have thought through the following issues beforehand.)

Agree on your purpose. Are you getting together to gain wisdom and direction for your lives? to finally get acquainted with the Bible? to support one another in following Christ? to encourage those who are exploring—or reexploring—the Church? for other reasons?

Agree on attitudes. For example: "We're all beginners here." "We're here to help each other understand and respond to God's word." "We're not here to offer counseling or direction to each other." "We want to read Scripture prayerfully." What do *you* wish to emphasize? Make it explicit!

Agree on ground rules. Barbara J. Fleischer, in her useful book *Facilitating for Growth,* recommends that a group clearly state its approach to the following:

- ◆ Preparation. Do we agree to read the material and prepare the questions before each meeting?
- ◆ Attendance. What kind of priority will we give to our meetings?
- ◆ Self-revelation. Are we willing to help the others in the group gradually get to know us—our weaknesses as well as our strengths, our needs as well as our gifts?
- ◆ Listening. Will we commit ourselves to listen to each other?
- ◆ Confidentiality. Will we keep everything that is shared *with* the group *in* the group?
- ◆ Discretion. Will we refrain from sharing about the faults and sins of people outside the group?
- ◆ Encouragement and support. Will we give as well as receive?
- ◆ Participation. Will we give each person time and opportunity to make a contribution?

You could probably take a pen and draw a circle around *listening* and *confidentiality*. Those two points are especially important.

The following items could be added to Fleischer's list:

◆ Relationship with parish. Is our group part of the adult faith formation program? independent but operating with the express approval of the pastor? not a parish-based group at all?

◆ New members. In the course of the six meetings, will new members be allowed to join?

Agree on housekeeping.

◆ When will we meet?

◆ How often will we meet? Meeting weekly or every other week is best if you can manage it. William Riley remarks, "Meetings once a month are too distant from each other for the threads of the last session not to be lost" *(The Bible Study Group: An Owner's Manual)*.

◆ How long will meetings run?

◆ Where will we meet?

◆ Is any setup needed? Christine Dodd writes that "the problem with meeting in a place like a church hall is that it can be very soul destroying" given the cold, impersonal feel of many church facilities. If you have to meet in a church facility, Dodd recommends doing something to make the area homey *(Making Scripture Work)*.

◆ Who will host the meetings? Leaders and hosts are not necessarily the same.

◆ Will we have refreshments? Who will provide them?

◆ What about childcare? Most experienced leaders of Bible discussion groups discourage bringing infants or other children to adult Bible discussions.

Agree on leadership. You need someone to facilitate— to keep the discussion on track, to see that everyone has a chance to speak, to help the group stay on schedule. Rena Duff, editor of the newsletter *Sharing God's Word Today,* recommends having two or three people take turns leading the discussions.

It's okay if the leader is not an expert regarding the Bible. You have this booklet, and if questions come up that no one can answer, you can delegate a participant to do a little research between meetings. It's important for the leader to set an example of listening, to draw out the quieter members (and occasionally restrain the more vocal ones), to move the group on when it gets stuck, to remind the members of their agreements, and to summarize what the group is accomplishing.

Bible discussion is an opportunity to experience the fulfillment of Jesus' promise "Where two or three are gathered in my name, I am there among them" (Matthew 18:20). Put your discussion group in Jesus' hands. Pray for the guidance of the Spirit. And have a great time exploring God's word together!

Suggestions for Individuals

You can use this booklet just as well for individual study as for group discussion. While discussing the Bible with other people can be a rich experience, there are advantages to individual reading. For example:

◆ You can focus on the points that interest you most.

◆ You can go at your own pace.

◆ You can be completely relaxed and unashamedly honest in your answers to all the questions, since you don't have to share them with anyone!

Our suggestions for using this booklet on your own are these:

◆ Don't skip "Questions to Begin." The questions can help you as an individual reader warm up to the topic of the reading.

◆ Take your time on "Questions for Careful Reading" and "Questions for Application." While a group will probably not have enough time to work on all the questions, you can allow yourself the time to consider all of them if you are using the booklet by yourself.

◆ After reading the "Guide to the Reading," go back and reread the Scripture text before answering the "Questions for Application."

◆ Take the time to look up all the parenthetical Scripture references.

◆ Read the entire section of John's Gospel from chapter 1 through chapter 10, not just the parts excerpted in this booklet. Your total understanding of John's Gospel will be increased by reading through the entire first half.

◆ Since you control the pace, give yourself plenty of opportunities to reflect on the meaning of the Gospel for you. Let your reading be an opportunity for these words to become God's words to you.

Resources

Bibles

The following editions of the Bible contain the full set of biblical
books recognized by the Catholic Church, along with a great deal
of useful explanatory material:

- ◆ The Catholic Study Bible (Oxford University Press), which
  uses the text of the New American Bible
- ◆ The Catholic Bible: Personal Study Edition (Oxford University
  Press), which also uses the text of the New American Bible
- ◆ The New Jerusalem Bible, the regular (not the reader's)
  edition (Doubleday)

Books

- ◆ George R. Beasley-Murray, *John* Word Biblical Commentary,
  vol. 36 (Nashville, Tenn.: Thomas Nelson Publishers, 1999).
- ◆ Raymond E. Brown, S.S., *The Gospel according to John (I–XII)*
  The Anchor Bible, vol. 29 (New York: Doubleday, 1966).
- ◆ Raymond E. Brown, S.S., *A Retreat with John the Evangelist:
  That You May Have Life* (Cincinnati, Ohio: St. Anthony
  Messenger Press, 1998).
- ◆ Francis J. Moloney, S.D.B., *The Gospel of John* Sacra Pagina
  Series, vol. 4 (Collegeville, Minn.: The Liturgical Press, 1998).
- ◆ Leo Zanchettin, ed., *John: A Devotional Commentary*
  (Ijamsville: Md.: The Word Among Us, 2000).

How has Scripture had an impact on your life? Was this booklet
helpful to you in your study of the Bible? Please send comments,
suggestions, and personal experiences to Kevin Perrotta c/o Trade
Editorial Department, Loyola Press, 3441 N. Ashland Ave.,
Chicago, IL 60657.